THE CATHOLIC PRIESTHOOD AND WOMEN

THE CATHOLIC PRIESTHOOD AND WOMEN

A Guide to the Teaching of the Church

Sara Butler, MSBT

HillenbrandBooks

Chicago / Mundelein, Illinois

Nihil Obstat
Reverend Anthony J. Brankin, STL
Censor Deputatus
October 27, 2006

Imprimatur
Reverend John F. Canary, STL, DMIN
Vicar General
Archdiocese of Chicago
October 30, 2006

The *Nihil Obstat* and *Imprimatur* are official declarations that a book is free of doctrinal and moral error. No implication is contained therein that those who have granted the *Nihil Obstat* and *Imprimatur* agree with the content, opinions, or statements expressed. Nor do they assume any legal responsibility associated with publication.

Hillenbrand Books is an imprint of Liturgy Training Publications (LTP) and the Liturgical Institute at the University of St. Mary of the Lake (USML). The imprint is focused on contemporary and classical theological thought concerning the liturgy of the Catholic Church. Available at bookstores everywhere, or through LTP by calling 1-800-933-1800 or visiting www.LTP.org. Further information about the **Hillenbrand Books** publishing program is available from the University of St. Mary of the Lake/Mundelein Seminary, 1000 East Maple Avenue, Mundelein IL 60060 (847-837-4542), on the Web at www.usml.edu/liturgicalinstitute, or e-mail litinst@usml.edu.

Printed in the United States of America.

Library of Congress Control Number: 2006937258

ISBN 978-1-59525-016-2

HCPW

Contents

Acknowledgments

The editor of *Voices*, Helen Hull Hitchcock, has kindly given
permission to reprint in chapter one some portions of my essay
"Ordination: Reviewing the Fundamental Reasons," from *Voices* XIX:3
(Michaelmas, 2004): 19–26.

The overall argument of this book appeared in "Women's Ordination
and the Development of Doctrine," *The Thomist* 61:4 (October 1997):
501–524. It was originally presented in The Millennium Lecture series
sponsored by St. Joseph's Church in Greenwich Village, New York.

Introduction

The Church does not have the authority to admit women to priestly ordination. This judgment, rendered by Pope John Paul II in 1994,[1] simply confirms a tradition observed in practice from apostolic times, but its authoritative reaffirmation troubles many. While they acknowledge that the Pope has the right and even the duty to intervene to protect the apostolic faith when controversy threatens the Church's unity,[2] many Catholics reject this particular judgment. For them, the exclusion of women from the priesthood is a clear injustice. They are supported by public opinion and encouraged in their dissent by theologians who are convinced that objections made to this teaching are solid, weighty, and persuasive. Those who dissent are frustrated by the official prohibition of further open debate. Other Catholics are scandalized by the ongoing opposition to papal teaching. The question continues to divide Catholics, then, even though the magisterium asserts that it has been officially, even infallibly, settled.[3]

A new generation has come of age since the papal reiteration of the traditional teaching in 1994. Young Catholic adults who are serious about the practice of their faith are puzzled, dismayed, and dis-edified by the distress and anger they encounter when the topic is aired. They did not live through the debate at its highest pitch, but they need to understand it. Seminarians among them will be required to profess publicly that they accept the Church's teaching, and they

---

1. See "Apostolic Letter on Ordination and Women," *Origins* 24:4 (June 9. 1994): 49.51–52, and "Doctrinal Congregation, Inadmissibility of Women to Ministerial Priesthood," *Origins* 25:24 (November 30, 1995): 401.403–405.

2. In 1973, the Congregation for the Doctrine of the Faith wrote: "The People of God has particular need of the intervention and assistance of the magisterium when internal disagreements arise and spread concerning a doctrine that must be believed or held, lest it lose the communion of the one faith in the one Body of the Lord (cf. Ephesians 4:45)." See *Mysterium ecclesiae (Declaration in Defense of the Catholic Doctrine on the Church against Certain Errors of the Present Day)*, 2 (Washington, D.C.: United States Catholic Conference, 1973).

3. See Avery Dulles' comparison, "*Humanae vitae* and *Ordinatio sacerdotalis:* Problems of Reception" in *Church Authority in American Culture* (New York: Crossroad, 1999), 14–28.

will be called on to explain it.[4] They need a theological orientation to the topic that engages the chief objections.

This book was written at the urging of many such young adults, chiefly seminarians at the University of St. Mary of the Lake's Mundelein Seminary in Mundelein, Illinois, and more recently at St. Joseph's Seminary ("Dunwoodie") in Yonkers, New York. It is shaped quite directly by their questions. It attempts to interpret and defend the Church's teaching, and at the same time to explain why many have had difficulty accepting it.[5]

The book has also been shaped by my own questions. For several years, I supported the movement for women's ordination to the Catholic priesthood. At the time I regarded this as a litmus test that would show whether or not there could be real equality between women and men in the Church. I failed to take into account the implications of Catholic teaching on the nature of Holy Orders as a sacrament. I concurred with the conclusion of a Task Force of the Catholic Theological Society of America (1978), which I chaired, that the available evidence favored the admission of women to priestly ordination, unless further examination of theological anthropology and the nature of "pastoral office" were to identify some obstacle that had been overlooked.[6] Later, however, through my participation in the Anglican-Roman Catholic Consultation in the United States and, as a consultant, on the Bishops' Committee for a Pastoral Letter on Women's Concerns, I became convinced that the feminist analysis of sexual complementarity and the theology of the ministerial priesthood adopted by CTSA Task Force were both seriously deficient.[7]

My remaining misgivings about the adequacy of the Church's teaching on women's full equality with men were put to rest by Pope John Paul II's "theology of the body" and his response to the feminist critique in the apostolic letter *Mulieris dignitatem* (1988). Then,

---

4. The profession includes this statement: "I also firmly accept and hold each and everything definitively proposed by the Church regarding teaching on faith and morals."

5. In this, it intends to supplement the pre-1994 work of Manfred Hauke, and the more strictly theological work of Benedict Ashley, Francis Martin, and Gerhard Ludwig Müller.

6. *Research Report: Women in Church and Society,* ed. Sara Butler (Bronx, New York: The Catholic Theological Society of America, 1978), 46–47.

7. See my "Second Thoughts on Ordaining Women," *Worship* 63:2 (March 1989): 157–65, for a more detailed report of these initial misgivings.

when given a second opportunity to review the question of women's ordination, this time with colleagues on the Anglican-Roman Catholic International Commission (ARCIC), I was led to see more clearly how the Catholic doctrine on this matter pertains to the constitution of the Church. This struck me as we worked together for consensus on the place of tradition in the discernment of doctrine, the relation of apostolic ministry and apostolic succession to the apostolic faith, the episcopal structure of the Church, and the role of the magisterium in the assessment of new questions.[8] In other words, I saw how the question of ordaining women raises again the contested issues of the Reformation. Those issues concern not the complementarity of the sexes but the constitution of the Church and the sacramentality of the priesthood.[9] Doctrinal presuppositions about them underlie the "fundamental reasons" that the magisterium gives for reserving the ministerial priesthood to men.

Is the ministerial priesthood rooted in Jesus' call of the Twelve? Did the Lord provide the Church with an apostolic ministry and intend that it be handed on to others? Are those ordained to the ministerial priesthood associated with the Lord's own service to the Church in a way distinct from that of the baptized? For Catholics, the answer to these questions is "yes." The teaching of the magisterium cannot be received if these questions are thought to remain open; they belong to the Church's "settled doctrine."[10]

The organization of this book reflects the path of my own intellectual and spiritual journey. It opens with an exposition the 1994 document *Ordinatio sacerdotalis* in which I call attention to the impact of differences inherited from the Reformation. Chapter two traces the development of doctrine that has taken place regarding the full equality of women and men in the social order and in the Church. Chapter three is pivotal. Here, I tackle the most common objections to

---

8. The members of ARCIC determined that discussion of the priestly ordination of women must be preceded by consensus on these questions; this consensus is reported in the Agreed Statement, *The Gift of Authority* (1999).

9. See my essays "The Ordination of Women: A New Obstacle to the Recognition of Anglican Orders," *Anglican Theological Review* 78 (Winter 1996): 96–113, and "Women's Ordination and the Development of Doctrine," *The Thomist* 61 (October 1997): 501–24.

10. *Catechism of the Catholic Church* (hereafter, CCC). See Francis A. Sullivan's study, *From Apostles to Bishops: The Development of the Episcopacy in the Early Church* (New York: The Newman Press, 2000) for a reassessment of some of the critical questions involved.

the Church's teaching. One of these rests on the failure to notice the difference between the fundamental reasons for the tradition and the theological arguments offered to elucidate it. I have treated these reasons and arguments in different chapters to underline the important distinction between them. Chapter six takes up, very briefly, some other well-known objections.

In chapter seven I review the controversy from the perspective of the development of doctrine. I argue that the admission of women to the Catholic priesthood cannot constitute an authentic development since it ultimately requires, I believe, a radical reconstruction or even denial of fundamental Catholic doctrines. Using a criterion of discernment identified by Cardinal Newman, I judge that it cannot be authentic. The magisterium's claim that the reservation of priestly ordination to men represents fidelity to the will of Christ, on the other hand, throws light on these doctrines and places them within a new, rich synthesis. The same criterion acknowledges this as evidence that it belongs to the apostolic tradition and is part of the deposit of the faith.

Many friends and colleagues have made significant contributions to my understanding of this topic. I wish to thank in a particular way the help of learned colleagues from the CTSA; the Bishops' Committee for a Pastoral Letter on Women's Concerns; the Institute for Ecumenical and Cultural Research in Collegeville, Minnesota; the Anglican-Roman Catholic Consultation in the United States; and the Anglican-Roman Catholic International Commission. Special thanks are due to the students, librarians, faculty, and administration at the University of St. Mary of the Lake, Mundelein Seminary (1989–2003), and at St. Joseph's Seminary, Dunwoodie (2003 to the present). In a particular way, I wish to acknowledge the help of Father Charles R. Meyer (Mundelein) and Monsignor Kevin O'Brien (St. Joseph's) for their critical reading of texts that prepared the way for this manuscript. I take full responsibility, of course, for its argument. Mr. Kevin Thornton has been an encouraging and enthusiastic editor. I owe the opportunity to study theology and participate in this important discussion to my religious congregation, the Missionary Servants of the Most Blessed Trinity. I am especially grateful to my sisters in religion, my poet friend Sue Dwyer, my sister Mary, and all the other members of my family who have lovingly supported me in my projects.

Abbreviations

CCC   *Catechism of the Catholic Church.* Second edition, 1997.

DS   H. Denzinger–A. Schönmetzer. *Enchiridion Symbolorum: Definitionum et Declarationum de rebus fidei et morum.* Thirty-second edition. Freiburg im Breisgau: Herder, 1963.

ND   J. Neuner–J. Dupuis. *The Christian Faith in the Doctrinal Documents of the Catholic Church.* Sixth revised and enlarged edition. New York: Alba House, 1996.

Chapter 1

The Church's Teaching and the Present Discussion

THE QUESTION: WHY RESERVE PRIESTHOOD TO MEN?

Why does the Catholic Church reserve priestly ordination to men? The question is asked by Catholics, by other Christians, especially our partners in ecumenical dialogue, and by many curious and often critical observers who do not share our faith. If we look for teaching documents from councils or Popes, we may be surprised to discover that this question was not directly addressed in an official way until our own times. This does not mean that theologians never entertained the question — some did, especially the Scholastic theologians of the Middle Ages. Even in the first centuries of the Christian era, a few Fathers of the Church, canonists, and commentators on ecclesiastical legislation gave it some attention. But the evidence of these witnesses has to be evaluated cautiously because they speak to situations quite remote from ours (for example, the practices of ancient heretical communities) or take for granted views on the relationship between the sexes the Church now rejects as unacceptable. Formal interventions of the magisterium, in fact, date only from the period following the Second Vatican Council (1962–1965), and from the pontificates of Paul VI (1964–1978) and John Paul II (1978–2005).

AN OFFICIAL ANSWER:
ORDINATIO SACERDOTALIS (1994)

The most authoritative magisterial response to the question was given by Pope John Paul II in *Ordinatio sacerdotalis (On Reserving Priestly Ordination to Men Alone)*,[1] an apostolic letter dated Pentecost Sunday, May 22, 1994, and addressed to his brother bishops. In this chapter we shall look closely at the text of this very short papal document in order to introduce its various elements and place them in the context of the contemporary discussion.

Its Bottom Line

First, let us take note of the "bottom line"—the conclusion of *Ordinatio sacerdotalis* (art. 4). After nearly three decades of theological debate about and public advocacy for the ordination of women to the Catholic priesthood, Pope John Paul II pronounces a solemn judgment: "the Church has no authority whatsoever to confer priestly ordination on women." He also directs that "this judgment is to be definitively held by all the Church's faithful." He explains that he exercises his apostolic authority in order to remove all doubt about the Church's teaching on a matter that pertains to her "divine constitution."

The apostolic letter does not propose this as a new doctrine but claims only to confirm—after a period in which it has been put in question—a teaching "preserved by the constant and universal tradition of the Church and firmly taught by the magisterium in its more recent documents."[2] From the outset of our examination we should notice the precise focus of this assertion: it concerns *the limits of the Church's authority over the sacrament of Holy Orders*.[3] What must be "definitively held" is that the Church does not have the authority to ordain women as priests. Catholics may no longer regard this as an open question or publicly advocate for a change in Church practice.

---

1. "Apostolic Letter on Ordination and Women," *Origins* 24:4 (June 9, 1994): 49. 51–52. For the text, all pertinent documentation, and supporting essays, see Congregation for the Doctrine of the Faith, *From "Inter Insigniores" to "Ordinatio Sacerdotalis": Documents and Commentaries* (Washington, D.C.: United States Catholic Conference, 1998), hereafter *From "Inter Insigniores."*

2. *Ordinatio sacerdotalis,* 4 (ND 1760).

3. We refer to the doctrine of "the priesthood," rather than of "Holy Orders," because we do not intend to consider whether this decision applies also to the diaconate.

But why? What is the reason for reserving priestly ordination to men? In the first three articles of *Ordinatio sacerdotalis* the Pope explains very concisely the basis for his judgment, namely, that the tradition of reserving priestly ordination to men can be traced to the will of Christ. Following the usual form of this sort of document, he begins by recounting the doctrine of previous statements of the magisterium. These, in turn, make reference to the evidence found in scripture and tradition. He then comments on these prior statements very succinctly in order to respond to some arguments commonly urged against them. Finally, he reaffirms the equal dignity of women in the Church and indicates the weight of the document itself.

Its Starting Point

In the very first sentence of *Ordinatio sacerdotalis,* Pope John Paul II asserts that "from the beginning" priestly ordination "has always been reserved to men alone" in the Catholic Church. He also specifies that priestly ordination "hands on the office entrusted by Christ to his Apostles of teaching, sanctifying, and governing the faithful." By saying this, he recalls the Church's faith—confidently proposed by the Second Vatican Council[4]—that the ministerial priesthood has its origin in Christ, was first entrusted to the apostles, is handed on by their successors, and confers on the person ordained the office of carrying out Christ's threefold ministry with respect to the rest of the faithful. According to Pope John Paul II, then, the starting point for a proper consideration of the issue is the doctrine of the ministerial priesthood, a doctrine that has a necessary reference to the Lord Jesus, the apostles, and their successors.

This doctrine of priesthood, as we shall see, determines the judgment of the Catholic Church concerning the possibility of ordaining women. The answer to the question "Why?" is bound up with the belief that Holy Orders is a sacrament instituted by Christ, that his intention for the priesthood is known by way of the mission he gave the Twelve, and that this office is passed on in apostolic succession. If the Church does not have the authority to change her

---

4. See *Lumen gentium* (*Dogmatic Constitution on the Church*), 18–21, 28, and *Presbyterorum ordinis* (*Decree on the Ministry and Life of Priests*), 2.

tradition regarding this, it is because the ministry is a gift which the Lord "entrusted to the Apostles" and which she is bound to preserve.

This teaching regarding the priesthood is not a new doctrine, and the reservation of priestly ordination to men is not a new practice. Prior to the post-conciliar controversy, the Catholic Church held this teaching so firmly that there was no need to define it.[5] The explanation given today has, however, a rather new focus—a focus that corresponds, in fact, to the challenge put in our time. According to this challenge, the Church's tradition of practice and the theology that justified it correspond to an outdated estimation of women. Both the practice and the theology need to be brought into line with contemporary teaching on the equal dignity of women with men. In other words, a development of doctrine is not only possible but also required. To this challenge, the Pope replies: the Church is not free— does not have the *authority*—to change this practice because it is rooted in the will of Christ. This conviction has been "preserved" in the tradition, even though, he acknowledges, it has been "firmly taught by the magisterium" only in its "more recent documents" (art. 4).

RECENT CHURCH DOCUMENTS AND SOME FEATURES OF THE DEBATE

The documents Pope John Paul II refers to were occasioned by two developments. One was the ordination of women in some parts of the Anglican Communion, and the other was the growth within the Catholic Church herself of an advocacy movement for women's ordination. These recent interventions of the magisterium are recalled both as testimony to the Church's perennial conviction and also as evidence that this conviction was carefully reconsidered in light of contemporary questions.

---

5. See *Inter insigniores*, 1. The magisterium felt no need "to intervene in order to formulate a principle which was not attacked, or to defend a law which was not challenged." This same tradition has been preserved unbroken by the Churches of the East. "Vatican Declaration: Women in Ministerial Priesthood," *Origins* 6:33 (February 3, 1977): 517, 519–524.

Pope Paul VI's Letter to the Archbishop of Canterbury

In July 1975, the Most Reverend F. Donald Coggan, the Archbishop of Canterbury and Primate of the Anglican Communion, wrote to Pope Paul VI to request "ecumenical counsel" regarding the matter of ordaining women to the priesthood. Dr. Coggan advised the Pope of the growing consensus among Anglicans that "there are no fundamental objections in principle" to the ordination of women as priests.[6] He asked for papal "counsel" in view of the progress the Anglican-Roman Catholic International Commission had already made toward a doctrinal agreement on ministry and ordination,[7] and in view of shared Catholic and Anglican hopes for the restoration of "full communion."

The first citation of the magisterium in *Ordinatio sacerdotalis*, then, is of Pope Paul's response to the Archbishop of Canterbury. In his letter (November 30, 1975), the Pope recalls that the Catholic Church holds "it is not admissible to ordain women to the priesthood, for very fundamental reasons." He identifies three: Christ's example of choosing only men as apostles (the argument from scripture), the Church's constant practice in imitation of the Lord (the argument from tradition), and the consistent teaching that this practice is "in accordance with God's plan for his Church" (the witness of the magisterium). The Pope's letter only states the reasons; it does not provide evidence for them or elucidate them by means of theological arguments.

The Wider Ecumenical Context

To appreciate the significance of this correspondence, and of the decision in some member Churches of the Anglican Communion to ordain women to the priesthood, it is necessary to know something of the larger ecumenical debate on the issue. The tradition of reserving priestly ordination to men has been unbroken in the Churches of East and West, which maintain a sacramental understanding of priesthood. Toward the middle of the twentieth century, however, a movement to

---

6. See "Letters Exchanged by Pope and Anglican Leader," *Origins* 6:9 (August 12, 1976): 129.131–132.

7. In 1973, the Commission produced the "Canterbury Statement," an Agreed Statement on Ministry and Ordination.

ordain women gained momentum among Protestant Christians.[8] At the time, Catholic theologians took little notice of this. They did not look upon the gradual admission of women to the ordained ministry in Protestant Churches as a breach in the constant tradition because they did not regard the Protestant ministry as belonging to that tradition. Neither, for that matter, did Protestants. The Reformers denied that Holy Orders is a sacrament and insisted that the Protestant "minister" was not a "priest" according to the Catholic understanding of that term. Ecumenical studies regularly acknowledged that most ecclesial families stemming from the Reformation had a "prophetic" model of ordained ministry that stood in clear contrast to the "priestly" model maintained in the Catholic and Orthodox Churches. Prior to the initiation of bilateral ecumenical dialogues involving the Catholic Church—that is, prior to the Second Vatican Council—Catholic theologians were relatively indifferent to the discussion of women's ordination among Protestants. They were confident that the office to which such women were admitted was the preaching ministry of the Reformation, not the Catholic priesthood.[9]

To grasp the way the controversy has unfolded, it is also useful to know that among Protestants themselves the debate about the ordination of women centered chiefly on the normative value of the New Testament teaching about women's status vis-à-vis men and their participation in the Church. In effect, what was contested was the interpretation of Saint Paul's teaching regarding the divine plan for relationships between men and women (the "order of creation")[10] and of the "Pauline ban" on women's teaching and exercising authority over men in the Church (1 Corinthians 14:33–35;[11] 1 Timothy 2:11–15). To those who agreed that the full equality of women with men could be satisfactorily defended by appeal to other New Testament texts such as Galatians 3:28 (in Christ there is no longer "male and female"),

---

8. See John E. Lynch, "The Ordination of Women: Protestant Experience in Ecumenical Perspective," *Journal of Ecumenical Studies* 12:2 (Spring 1975): 173–197.

9. See Kathleen Bliss, *The Service and Status of Women in the Churches* (London: S.C.M. Press, 1952), 136.

10. See 1 Corinthians 11:3–9 and Ephesians 5:22–24.

11. Many exegetes regard verse 34 as an interpolation.

it seemed that no biblical objection to women's ordination remained.[12] Elements more directly linked to the Catholic doctrine of the priesthood (for example, the call of the Twelve, the representation of Christ, and apostolic succession) did not factor heavily in the discussions and were not generally thought to be decisive.

Developments in the Anglican Communion

The situation among the Anglicans, however, was more complex because of their traditional esteem for a high, or "Catholic," view of ordained ministry. The Second Vatican Council had affirmed the "special place" of the Anglican Communion among the separated Christians in the West and recognized that many Catholic traditions and institutions continued to exist within it.[13] By the 1970s, an official bilateral dialogue was underway, and hopes were high for an eventual reconciliation of ministries. The successful completion by the Anglican-Roman Catholic International Commission of an Agreed Statement on Ministry and Ordination in 1973 encouraged the belief that Anglicans did, in fact, intend to ordain their clergy as "priests" in the Catholic tradition.[14]

Once some provinces of the Anglican Communion began to admit woman to the priesthood, then, the issue was raised in a new way for Catholics. It was no longer only a matter of admitting women to the preaching ministry of the Reformation; the Anglican bishops' intention was to confer the priesthood on women. At the time many Catholic theologians took Paul VI's reply to the Archbishop of Canterbury to be no more than the formal restatement of a tradition that clearly needed further investigation, but the Pope's own letter warned that the ordination of Anglican women as priests would introduce "an element of grave difficulty" into the dialogue between the two communions.

---

12. Krister Stendahl's classic study, *The Bible and the Role of Women* (Philadelphia: Fortress, 1966), explains how the debate proceeded in the (Lutheran) Church of Sweden in the 1950s.

13. *Unitatis redintegratio (Decree on Ecumenism)*, 13.

14. The 1979 "Elucidation" (art. 5) explains that because the ordination of women had not been a point of division in the sixteenth century, it was not addressed. See my assessment, "The Ordination of Women: A New Obstacle to the Recognition of Anglican Orders," *Anglican Theological Review*, 78 (Winter 1996): 96–113.

There is one further point to note concerning the Pope's letter to Archbishop Coggan. It is this: the "fundamental reasons" he supplied were not those commonly understood to explain the position of the Catholic Church. At the time, Catholic theologians were reconsidering the scriptural evidence and investigating whether the tradition might actually have been shaped by historically conditioned views of women's nature. They were critical of Saint Thomas Aquinas's explanation that women were excluded because they were unable, by reason of their sex, to "signify eminence." The Pope did not cite either the Pauline texts or Saint Thomas's explanation. He appealed instead to the Gospels (Christ's example of choosing only men as apostles), the tradition (the Church's constant practice, in imitation of the Lord), and the magisterium (the consistent teaching that this practice is "in accord with God's plan for his Church").

The Declaration *Inter Insigniores*

The evidence supporting the Pope's response to the Archbishop of Canterbury was laid out the following year. He directed the Congregation of the Doctrine of the Faith to explain the tradition more fully, not only for the sake of our ecumenical dialogue partners but also to guide—and to curb—the increasingly vigorous debate within the Catholic Church. The Congregation produced *Inter insigniores* (the *Declaration on the Question of the Admission of Women to the Ministerial Priesthood*). Paul VI having given his approval and ordered its promulgation, the declaration was released on January 27, 1977, although dated the previous October 15, the feast day of Saint Teresa of Avila. It is the second document cited by John Paul II in *Ordinatio sacerdotalis*.

Inter insigniores, echoing the Pope's letter to the Archbishop of Canterbury, also appealed to the tradition itself as something that the Church cannot alter because it is rooted in the example and will of Christ. According to the declaration, it is "necessary to recall that the Church, in fidelity to the example of the Lord, *does not consider herself authorized* to admit women to priestly ordination."[15] *Inter insigniores* (arts. 1–4) sets out quite fully the "fundamental

---

15. *Inter insigniores,* introduction (emphasis added).

reasons" for this judgment. In support of the tradition the declaration offers "theological arguments" from the analogy of faith[16] (arts. 5–6). In *Ordinatio sacerdotalis*, Pope John Paul mentions *Inter insigniores* but does not specify its contents. We shall summarize them here, and save a fuller exposition for chapters three and four.

The declaration lays out the "fundamental reasons" for the Church's judgment in four articles. The reasons are 1) that there is an unbroken, universal tradition of admitting only men to ministerial priesthood; 2) that this tradition is rooted in Christ's manner of acting, that is, his choice of men as his apostles; 3) that this tradition was maintained by the apostles in fidelity to his example; and 4) that this tradition is normative for the Church.

What are these arguments? The declaration distinguishes these "fundamental reasons" from the "theological arguments" supplied to support them. The latter, also called "arguments from fittingness," are offered to elucidate why the Lord's choice of men and not women is appropriate, and not discriminatory against women. Most popular expositions of Catholic teaching on this matter overlook the "fundamental reasons" and offer instead reasoning drawn from the "theological arguments." It is important to realize, therefore, that the authority of the declaration's teaching is attached to the "fundamental reasons" and not to the "theological arguments."

First, there are arguments related to the mystery of Christ: these address the question of sacramental symbolism and, related to it, the theological relevance of Jesus' maleness, for example, the argument that only a male can act *in persona Christi*. Second, there are arguments related to the mystery of the Church. These address the nature of the Church, the equality of the baptized, and the place of the ministerial priesthood in the Church.

Pope Paul VI's "Angelus Address"

Ordinatio sacerdotalis concludes its brief account of the teaching of *Inter insigniores* with reference to a comment Pope Paul VI made in his Angelus Address "On the Role of Women in the Plan of Salvation" on January 30, 1977—three days after the declaration's publication.

---

16. These are arguments advanced by drawing out the implications of other doctrines. I will enclose these two expressions in quotation marks to draw attention to this distinction.

The "real reason" for the Church's tradition, he said at the time, is the will of Christ regarding "the constitution of the Church" and "her theological anthropology."[17] According to Pope Paul, then, this question concerns more than a matter of sacramental discipline; it is linked to very fundamental Catholic doctrines. Later, the magisterium would teach that this tradition "pertains to the deposit of faith" in such a way that its denial endangers other articles of Catholic belief.

Inter Insigniores: The Problem of Reception

Inter insigniores did not settle the question of women's ordination but only fueled further debate within the Catholic community. The numerous changes the Council introduced, the social and political impact of liberal feminism, and a general optimism about progress in ecumenical dialogue—taken together—created a climate in which many thought it reasonable to ask whether the Catholic Church might not "modify her discipline and admit women to priestly ordination."[18] The favorable consideration of this possibility was encouraged by the study Haye van der Meer made under the direction of the prominent Jesuit theologian Karl Rahner in 1962.[19] Van der Meer undertook a comprehensive review of the historical evidence and theological argumentation on the ordination of women. Having retrieved from the Church's past an impressive collection of texts that betrayed a very negative evaluation of women, he speculated that misogynist views like these might ultimately account for the Church's practice. It is possible, he concluded, that the exclusion of women from the priesthood is not a genuinely theological tradition but only a customary way of acting dictated by sociocultural considerations.

Van der Meer's scholarly hypothesis, and the evidence he assembled to support it, affected the way many Catholics received *Inter insigniores.* To advocates of women's ordination, Pope Paul's appeal to another line of argument and the theological reasoning of the Congregation for the Doctrine of the Faith (1977) did not seem to

---

17. "Women in the Plan of God," *The Pope Speaks,* 22 (1977): 124–25.

18. *Inter insigniores,* introduction.

19. *Women Priests in the Catholic Church?* (Philadelphia: Temple University Press, 1973; German original, *Priestertum der Frau?,* 1969). Van der Meer has retracted his thesis in "De vrouw en hot priesterschap" (International), *Communio,* 14 (January 1989): 72–76.

be germane. Instead, it seemed to them that the tradition of reserving priestly ordination to men was closely tied to a faulty estimate of women. That being so, it appeared logical to assume that initiatives taken to improve women's status in the social order and in the Church would bring about a change in practice, a change requiring only a disciplinary relaxation or at most a rather straightforward development of doctrine.

Proponents of change were encouraged when the newly established international Synod of Bishops, at its 1971 assembly, asked that the Church's own witness to justice with respect to women be thoroughly examined and urged the Pope to create an international commission for this purpose. In 1972, the United States Bishops' Conference published a report by its doctrine commission, *Theological Reflections on the Ordination of Women*, which favored the traditional practice, but also acknowledged that serious study of some aspects of the issue had only begun. Other parties—bilateral ecumenical commissions, task forces, and advocacy groups—were highly optimistic about the possibility of a change. Several prominent Catholic theologians[20] publicly expressed the opinion that there were no theological reasons to prohibit women from being ordained priests. All of this contributed to the impression that the matter was open for review and possible development.

At the same time, the question of women's status and women's rights was receiving sustained attention worldwide: the United Nations had designated 1975 as International Women's Year. Pope Paul VI gave several public addresses related to this celebration. In the course of an address to the Holy See's International Study Commission on the Role of Women in Society and in the Church, he expressed, almost parenthetically, the reason he would continue to advance as the basis for the Church's practice: "Although women do not receive the call to the apostolate of the Twelve and therefore to the ordained ministries, they are nonetheless invited to follow Christ as disciples and co-workers. . . . We cannot change what our Lord did, nor his call to women."[21]

---

20. For example, Hans Küng, Karl Rahner, and Edward Schillebeeckx.

21. See Pope Paul VI, "Women/Disciples and Co-workers," *Origins* 4:45 (May 1, 1975): 718–719, at 719.

The Pope's judgment appeared to be challenged when in July 1976 the draft of a Pontifical Biblical Commission report on the role of women in the Bible was made available—without authorization—to the press.[22] The Commission members confirmed, on the one hand, that the New Testament undeniably attests to "the masculine character of the hierarchical order which has structured the Church since its beginning." But they concluded, on the other, that the New Testament alone could not settle once and for all "the problem of the possible accession of women to the presbyterate." This report sustained in many the belief that the question was still open for Catholics.

During the period immediately following *Inter insigniores,* scholars examined its every assertion and produced many studies, most of which were directed at offering alternative explanations and conclusions. Many of the critical studies do not engage the declaration's reasoning on its own terms. They tend to regard the "fundamental reasons" as impossible to establish on the basis of critical scholarship and to focus instead on refuting the "theological arguments"—as if these had been intended to bear the whole weight of the teaching. Some of these studies call into question points of settled doctrine having to do with Holy Orders and the constitution of the Church. Only one comprehensive study and a few collections of essays appeared in support of the declaration.[23]

Pope John Paul II's Letter, *Mulieris Dignitatem*

In *Ordinatio sacerdotalis* (art. 2), Pope John Paul II notes the conclusion of *Inter insigniores.* He does not repeat the "theological arguments," but calls attention instead to the importance of "Christ's way of acting," namely, his freedom in choosing the Twelve. In reiterating this point, he cites a passage from his apostolic letter *Mulieris dignitatem* (*On the Dignity and Vocation of Women,* 1988).[24] The passage recalls the sovereign freedom with which the Lord broke

---

22. "Can Women be Priests?" *Origins* 6:6 (July 1, 1976): 92–96.

23. Manfred Hauke, *Women in the Priesthood? A Systematic Analysis in the Light of the Order of Creation and Redemption,* (San Francisco: Ignatius Press, 1988), *The Order of the Priesthood: Nine Commentaries on the Vatican* (Huntington, Indiana: Our Sunday Visitor, 1978), and *The Church and Women,* ed. Helmut Moll (San Francisco: Ignatius Press, 1988).

24. "John Paul II/'Mulieris dignitatem,' On the Dignity and Vocation of Women," *Origins* 18:17 (October 6, 1988): 261.263–283.

with the customs, traditions, and laws of his time in relating to women. He reasons that Christ likewise acted freely in choosing only men to belong to the Twelve. One cannot grant his freedom with respect to these norms and then hope to demonstrate that he excluded women from apostolic ministry as a concession to these same norms. Freedom in the one case argues for freedom in the other.

In *Mulieris dignitatem,* the Pope provides a rather extensive "meditation" on Catholic teaching related to the whole question. He elaborates not only on the "fundamental reasons" offered by *Inter insigniores* but also on the "theological arguments" from fittingness, drawing forward in a particular way the logic of the nuptial metaphor (Christ the Bridegroom and the Church as Bride) in relation to the Eucharist, the celebration of the New Covenant. In *Ordinatio sacerdotalis,* however, this line of argumentation is referenced only by way of a footnote, note five.

Some Key Assertions of
Ordinatio Sacerdotalis

In his recapitulation of this recent teaching, then, Pope John Paul II focuses on Christ's sovereign freedom in choosing 12 men, a choice that the Church has always taken to be a norm for the ministerial priesthood. He reiterates the Church's belief that this plan does not contradict the Church's teaching on the dignity of women or constitute unjust discrimination against them. Finally, he announces that this teaching is to be definitively held.

Christ's Call of the Apostles Established the Norm

Ordinatio sacerdotalis (art. 2) emphasizes some important doctrinal considerations related to the call of the apostles. The Lord's choice, it asserts, "did not proceed from sociological or cultural motives peculiar to his time." Jesus' choice of the Twelve was made freely, he notes, after prayer. The call can be understood as a Trinitarian event: the Son chose "those whom he willed" in union with the Father and "through the Holy Spirit." Because this choice reflects "God's eternal plan" it cannot be dismissed as a historically conditioned decision open to subsequent development. In fact, the Church has always recognized that the Lord's example in choosing the men who became the foundation of the Church (see Revelation 21:4) provides a perennial norm in the matter of admitting candidates to the ministerial priesthood.

The consequences of this choice are also emphasized: these 12 men were not simply given a function that any member of the Church might later fulfill. Rather, they were drawn into a specific and intimate association with Christ; they were given the "mission of representing Christ the Lord and Redeemer." Not only they, but also those fellow workers to whom they would entrust this ministry (see 1 Timothy 3:1 ff.; 2 Timothy 1:6; Titus 1:5), and all who succeed the apostles in their mission, were included in this choice.

The themes given new prominence in this elaboration are drawn from the Church's traditional doctrine regarding Holy Orders, namely, that it has its origin in Christ's gift to the Twelve and is handed on by apostolic succession, that the functions it confers are not entrusted to all of the baptized, and that the mission entrusted to the ordained includes that of representing the Lord. Footnotes citing *Lumen gentium* (arts. 20 and 21) recall the teaching of the Second Vatican Council that the bishops are called to "take the place of Christ himself, teacher, shepherd and priest, and act in his person."[25] The footnotes also recall the Council's teaching on the analogy between the apostolic college and the episcopal college, a connection that plays an important part in the passage in the *Catechism of the Catholic Church*, § 1577, also cited in a footnote, which deals with the reservation of the ministerial priesthood to men:

> The Lord Jesus chose men *(viri)* to form the college of the twelve apostles, and the apostles did the same when they chose collaborators to succeed them in their ministry. The college of bishops, with whom the priests are united in the priesthood, makes the college of the twelve an ever-present and ever-active reality until Christ's return. The Church recognizes herself to be bound by this choice made by the Lord himself. For this reason the ordination of women is not possible.

---

25. *Lumen gentium*, 21. Documents of the Second Vatican Council are cited in the translation edited by Austin Flannery, *Vatican Council II: Constitutions, Decrees, Declarations*. Northport, New York: Costello Publishing Company, 1996).

The Divine Plan Does Not Contradict the Dignity of Women

According to *Ordinatio sacerdotalis* (art. 3), the Church's dispensation in this matter observes the plan of God's wisdom and must not be construed as discriminating against women. The Blessed Virgin's dignity was not compromised because she was not called to apostolic office and the ministerial priesthood; neither does the non-admission of other women to priestly ordination tell against their dignity. As female saints throughout the history of the Church bear witness, women share in the apostolic mission of the whole people of God and exemplify the holiness of the faithful to which the ministerial priesthood is ordered. In this context, the Pope recalls the admonition of *Inter Insigniores* (art. 6) that the highest place in the kingdom of heaven belongs not to the ministers but to the saints.

This Teaching Is to Be Definitively Held

Because the teaching preserved by the Church's constant and universal tradition and firmly taught by the contemporary magisterium continues to be called into question, the Pope declares—in virtue of his ministry of "confirming the brethren" (Luke 22:32)—that the Church does not have the authority to ordain women to the priesthood and directs that "this judgment is to be definitively held by all the faithful." This judgment itself, however, provoked further discussion and theological dissent. In October 1995, in response to a formal query about the status of *Ordinatio sacerdotalis,* the Congregation for the Doctrine of the Faith replied that its teaching belongs to the deposit of the faith and that it requires a definitive assent "since, founded on the written Word of God and from the beginning constantly preserved and applied in the Tradition of the Church, it has been set forth infallibly by the ordinary and universal magisterium."[26]

AN INITIAL ANALYSIS

Advocacy for the ordination of women in the twentieth century has been closely connected with the women's movement. Because the

---

26. "Doctrinal Congregation, 'Inadmissibility of Women to Ministerial Priesthood,'" *Origins* 25:24 (1995): 401.

ordained ministry of the Christian Churches is one of the professions traditionally reserved to men, the question of women's admission to ordination arose quite naturally once women began to claim equal rights with men. As we have pointed out, among Protestants the debate over admitting women to the ordained ministry was generally settled—for or against—by appeal to Saint Paul's teaching on the status of women in the economy of salvation. Some determined by a careful investigation of the scriptures that Paul's teaching, especially in Galatians 3:28, supports the view that women have equal rights and dignity with men not only before God but also in the social order and in the Church; they concluded that there was no "biblical obstacle" to their ordination. Given the prevailing theories of ordination and ministry among Protestants, they regarded baptismal equality as sufficient to establish that qualified women could be ordained to the Church's ministry.

The reinterpretation of New Testament texts was reached, in part, on the grounds that some of Saint Paul's admonitions for women's conduct within marriage and in the Church simply reflected the religious and sociocultural presuppositions of his time concerning the status of women. When Anglican and Catholic scholars began to review the evidence from the tradition, they asked whether the Fathers of the Church and the Scholastic Doctors might not also have been influenced more by the dictates of their culture than by Gospel principles when they maintained and defended the practice of reserving ordination to men. If the tradition of reserving priestly ordination to men represented only an unexamined practice rooted in a sociocultural estimation of women's incapacity for certain offices and leadership tasks, as van der Meer suggested, there would be no theological obstacle to the ordination of women to the priesthood.

Informed by Church-commissioned studies that spanned 50 years, the Anglican bishops who assembled at the 1968 Lambeth Conference judged that the scriptural evidence was inconclusive, and that the patristic and medieval explanations of the tradition were compromised by outmoded assumptions about women's inferior status and appropriate social roles. In their judgment, the simple lack of precedent was not sufficient to constitute a theological obstacle. Anglican provinces that subsequently voted in favor of women priests generally accept this reasoning. In their view, this is a matter of discipline that must now, in justice, be changed in order to acknowledge the equal dignity of women.

Catholic advocates for the ordination of women to the priesthood also framed the question in terms of the status of women and argued for it as a matter of equal rights for women in the Church. Given that the Second Vatican Council had condemned discrimination on the basis of sex with respect to basic human rights in the social order[27] and denied that there is any discrimination on the basis of sex in the Church,[28] it seemed to them reasonable to expect that a "development of doctrine" would lead to the ordination of women as priests. In *Ordinatio sacerdotalis*, however, the magisterium clearly sets forth its judgment that the Church has no authority to change the constant tradition of reserving priestly ordination to men. It teaches that this tradition represents fidelity to the will of Christ, who instituted the priesthood when he entrusted to the apostles his own office as priest, teacher, and pastor.

Ordinatio sacerdotalis takes as its starting point the Catholic doctrine of the ministerial priesthood. Advocates for change, however, typically frame the question in terms of the status and rights of women and of the baptized. Because this is their concrete starting point, we will take this up next. The evidence shows that the contemporary magisterium is firmly committed to the equal rights and dignity of women with men in the social order and in the Church.

---

27. See *Gaudium et spes (Pastoral Constitution on the Church in the Modern World)*, 29.
28. See *Lumen gentium*, 31, citing Galatians 3:28.

Chapter 2

The Status of Women in Society and in the Church

According to Peter Steinfels, over 60 percent of American Catholics now favor the ordination of women, "and for many of them the church's unwillingness to ordain women priests contradicts its own declared belief in the equality of all and the right of all to full participation in the church's life."[1] They presume that the Church's objection to the ordination of women is rooted in an outdated view of women and the "social roles" appropriate to them. In the shorthand used in this debate, they trace the problem to a "faulty anthropology."

Given these perceptions, it is important to review what the Catholic Church teaches regarding the status of women. We will begin by tracing a development that belongs to the tradition of Catholic social teaching. Next, we will see how that teaching has been implemented in the Church, in particular in the 1983 Code of Canon Law and with respect to the non-ordained ministries and Christian marriage.

WOMEN'S EQUAL RIGHTS IN THE SOCIAL ORDER

There has been a significant development in the Church's understanding of the fundamental rights of women and their full equality, as persons, with men. This development belongs to the tradition of Catholic social teaching, and can be traced from the nineteenth century to the Second Vatican Council (1962–1965). It took place quite apart from the question of women's access to the ministerial priesthood, for it was formulated in response to political ideologies, philosophical and

---

1. *A People Adrift: The Crisis of the Roman Catholic Church in America* (New York: Simon and Schuster, 2003), 293.

ethical systems, various feminist theories, and changing conditions in public life.

Prior to the 1940s, papal social teaching addressed the status of women only indirectly. It defended women's "special prerogatives" in the family: their "place" in the home and their work in the family circle. As women gained greater access to public life, the Popes encouraged Catholic women to participate in the Church's mission as agents of moral and social reform and became more unambiguously supportive of their entry into the political process. In response to challenges from liberal and radical feminism, though, papal teaching reaffirmed women's "role"—their dignity and duties as wives and mothers. It was not until the pontificate of Pius XII that serious attention was paid to women as "persons"—individuals with the same human and civil rights as men.[2] From then on, and especially following the Second Vatican Council, papal teaching has repeatedly affirmed women's equal rights with men in the social order.

Papal Teaching before the Second Vatican Council

The development of papal teaching on women's status was provoked by a series of challenges that had concrete as well as theoretical implications. Pope Leo XIII (1878–1903) looked on the Marxist-socialist proposal to "free" women from dependence on their fathers and husbands by urging their entry into the workforce as a grave threat to the father-headed family and the rights accruing to it as the fundamental cell of society. When Leo emphasized a wife's duty to her husband and children, he did so to safeguard the family as a social institution—not to keep married women in "bondage." When he protested a reorganization of the economy that would force women into the workplace, and demanded instead that men receive a "family wage," it was to protect women's right to raise their children in their own homes—not to confine them to the domestic sphere against their will. Likewise, when the popes of the early twentieth century urged protective legislation for working women, they were concerned more to counter the exploitation of their labor and defend them from sexual harassment in the workplace than to prevent women from participating

---

2. This analysis is from Robert Harahan, *The Vocation of Women: The Teaching of the Modern Popes from Leo XIII to Paul VI* (Rome: Pontificia Universitas Laterensis, 1983).

in public life. When they admonished women to honor and obey
their husbands (and husbands to respect and provide for their wives),
their intention was to defend the sanctity and stability of marriage,
in conscious opposition to forms of feminism that encouraged "free
love," contraception, abortion, and divorce.

In their social teaching, the Popes presupposed a specifically
feminine identity, deduced from woman's traditional roles of wife
and mother. Their concern was to repudiate innovations in the social
order that threatened to disrupt the family and undermine the stability
of marriage, not to reevaluate the status of women vis-à-vis men. Once
they came to appreciate the powerful moral influence women could
have in public life, however, the Popes began to promote Catholic
women's organizations in order to offset the impact of secular feminism.
They encouraged both married and single women to participate in
organized Catholic Action. They supported higher education for women
and their involvement not only in social reform and charity work but
also in the realm of culture and politics. Pope Pius XI (1922–1939),
countered feminist criticism by pointing to the Church's promotion of
women's religious life and its extensive contributions to society. He
insisted that the Church endorses the authentic promotion of women.

To meet the persistent accusation that the Catholic Church
was hostile to women's liberation, Pope Pius XII (1939–1958) turned
his attention more directly to women themselves, as responsible
persons who have different roles from men but are equal to them in
dignity. He eventually came to identify "personhood"—rather than
motherhood—as the foundation of women's dignity. His many
addresses to and about women take note of their diverse situations, for
example, the single women with a career, the mother who works outside
as well as inside the home, the women involved in Catholic Action
who bring the Gospel to bear on the culture, and women who take
direct part in social and political life.[3]

---

3. "Woman's Duties in Social and Political Life" (October 21, 1945), cited from William B.
Faherty, *The Destiny of Modern Woman in the Light of Papal Teaching* (Westminster, Maryland:
Newman Press, 1950), 109.

The Second Vatican Council and
Post-Conciliar Papal Teaching

Pope John XXIII (1958–1963) carried forward this new attention to
the authentic promotion of women as persons in his social teaching.
His sensitivity to the vocation of women and their right to personal
development, not only in the family but also in public life, is expressed
in his encyclical *Pacem in terris* (*Peace on Earth*, 1963): "Since women
are becoming ever more conscious of their human dignity, they will
not tolerate being treated as mere material instruments, but demand
rights befitting a human person both in domestic and public life."[4]
He recognized women's demand for "rights befitting a human person"
as one of the "signs of the times" that the Church needed to address.

It is under this rubric—the legitimate demand for the
recognition of rights belonging to the person—that the Second Vatican
Council treats the problem of discrimination on the basis of sex.
According to the Council, when it comes to human rights, the governing principle is theological: all human beings are radically equal as
persons because they are created in God's image (Genesis 1:27). This
principle is stated in *Gaudium et spes:*

> All women and men [*homines*, human beings] are endowed with a rational
> soul and are created in God's image; they have the same nature and origin
> and, being redeemed by Christ, they enjoy the same divine calling and
> destiny; there is here a basic equality between all and it must be accorded
> ever greater recognition.[5]

On the basis of this principle, and with respect to fundamental
human rights, the Council proceeds to denounce discrimination on
the grounds of sex:

> Undoubtedly not all people [*homines*] are alike as regards physical capacity
> and intellectual and moral powers. But any kind of social or cultural
> discrimination in basic personal rights on the grounds of sex, race, color,
> social conditions, language or religion, must be curbed and eradicated
> as incompatible with God's design.

---

4. *Pacem in terris (Peace on Earth)*, 41. The "rights" the Church upholds are the rights
bestowed by creation. See Joseph Ratzinger, "The Male Priesthood: A Violation of Women's
Rights?" in *From Inter Insigniores*, 142–150.

5. *Gaudium et spes*, 29.

Gaudium et spes (art. 29) illustrates discrimination of this sort by reference to the case of "women who are denied the chance freely to choose a husband, or a state of life, or to have access to the same educational and cultural benefits as are available to men." With respect to culture, it affirms that women "ought to be permitted to play their part fully" in all spheres of life "according to their nature."[6] The Council considers women not only in terms of their "place" in the home, or their unique and indispensable "role" in the family, but also in terms of their identity as "persons," subjects of personal rights and responsibilities in the human community.

Pope Paul VI repeatedly affirmed the Council's teaching on justice for women. In his first address to the International Study Commission on Women in Society and in the Church, he clearly expressed this:

> What is most urgent, at present, from all evidence, is the immense work of awakening and of promoting woman at the grass roots, in civil society, as well as in the church. It is the task that we ourselves strongly stressed . . . to labor everywhere to have discovered, respected and protected the rights and prerogatives of every woman in her life—educational, professional, civic, social, religious—whether single or married.[7]

In a subsequent address, Paul VI explicitly affirmed that creation in the divine image is the basis for the equality between the sexes: "God has created the human person, man and woman, in a single plan of love; he created the human being in his own image. Men and women are therefore equal before God: equal as persons, equal as children of God, equal in dignity, and equal also in their rights."[8]

Pope John Paul II, also drawing on the teaching of the Council, carried forward this vigorous defense of women's basic social, economic, and political rights and their equal dignity with men. It is evident from the clarifications he offered, moreover, that he was responding to the "feminist critique." In his apostolic letter *Mulieris dignitatem*, the Pope applied to women the Council's teaching on the dignity of the person: a person, made in the divine image, is "the

---

6. *Gaudium et spes*, 60.

7. "Women/Disciples and Co-Workers," 719.

8. "Women/Balancing Rights and Duties," *Origins* 5:35 (February 19, 1976): 449.551–552, at 551.

only creature on earth willed by God for its own sake."[9] A woman, no less than a man, is a person, endowed with intelligence and freedom and capable of self-determination. A woman is equal to a man as a person, "as a rational and free creature capable of knowing God and loving him."[10] A person, unlike lower forms of creation, can never be used, can never be treated as a thing or an object but must always be treated as a subject. Women, therefore, do not exist to serve the needs and interests of men. The Pope denounces the victimization of women by a mentality that considers the human being as an "object"—to be used, bought and sold, as an instrument for selfish pleasure. He repeatedly issued condemnations of discrimination, injustice, exploitation, and violence directed against women.[11]

Not content to condemn discrimination against women, John Paul II also actively promoted their cause. Addressing all the women of the world on the occasion of the Fourth World Conference on Women in Beijing in 1995, he wrote that justice for women requires "equal pay for equal work, protection for working mothers, fairness in career advancement, equality of spouses with regard to family rights and the recognition of everything that is part of the rights and duties of citizens in a democratic state."[12] Again, he asserted that "there should be no doubt that on the basis of their equal dignity with men 'women must have a full right to become actively involved in all areas of public life.'"[13] In his campaign for the authentic promotion of women, he pledged the Church to "an option in favor of girls and young women . . . especially the poorest."[14] He urged the creation of "a culture of equality"[15] in which women have full access to education, health care, culture, and the world of work, and in which women can participate and exercise leadership in all facets of public life.

---

9. *Gaudium et spes*, 24.

10. *Mulieris dignitatem*, 7.

11. See *Christifideles laici (On the Vocation and Mission of the Lay Faithful in the Church and in the World)*, 49, and *Pope John Paul II on the Genius of Women* (Washington, D.C.: USCC, 1997).

12. "Letter to Women," *Origins* 25:9 (July 27, 1995).

13. "Welcome to Gertrude Mongella," *Genius of Women*, 41.

14. "Letter to Mary Ann Glendon and the Holy See's Delegation to the Fourth World Conference on Women," *Genius of Women*, 60.

15. "Culture of Equality Is Urgently Needed Today" (June 25, 1995), *Genius of Women*, 22.

In July 2004, the Congregation for the Doctrine of the Faith issued a *Letter to the Bishops of the Catholic Church on the Collaboration of Men and Women in the Church and in the World*. The Congregation reaffirms the recent papal teaching when it urges "that women should be present in the world of work and in the organization of society, and that women should have access to positions of responsibility which allow them to inspire the policies of nations and to promote innovative solutions to economic and social problems."[16] The letter explicitly advocates the participation of women on the grounds that they are able to contribute a certain "humanizing" influence.

As these official texts show, there has been a gradual clarification and development in Catholic social teaching. The earlier concern to protect women's "place" in the home and their "role" in the family is now augmented by specific attention to women as "persons" having equal rights and equal dignity with men in the social order. From Pope John XXIII forward, the magisterium has increasingly expressed advocacy for women's full participation in public life and has vigorously denounced whatever would prevent this.

Papal Teaching on "False Equality"

By reason of this papal advocacy of women's human and civil rights in recent years, the Catholic Church may appear to be a new but strong ally of liberal feminism.[17] A close reading of the texts, however, reveals a significant philosophical difference. While liberal feminism insists that justice requires the identical treatment of women and men, the magisterium asserts that justice allows for and sometimes requires their differential treatment.[18] This is why Catholic texts speak not only of equal rights but also of equal "dignity."[19] Equal "dignity" refers to the fact that women and men, despite the differences between

---

16. "Vatican Doctrinal Congregation: Letter on the Collaboration of Men and Women," (*Origins* 34:11 [August 26, 2004]: 169.171–176), 13.

17. Because feminism has multiple expressions, it is necessary to specify "liberal feminism." See Sandra Schneiders, *Beyond Patching: Faith and Feminism in the Catholic Church*, revised edition (New York: Paulist Press, 2004), 18–25.

18. The principle of justice requires that equals be treated equally and what is different differently.

19. See *The Theology of the Body according to John Paul II: Human Love in the Divine Plan* (Boston: Pauline Books and Media, 1997), 45–48, for more on the value of sexual difference.

them, have equal worth or value. To respect women as persons means to respect their sexual identity.

According to Catholic social teaching, then, a program of equal rights for women that ignores the "special prerogatives" of those who are mothers would be unjust. Disregard for sexual difference, Pope Paul VI taught, leads to a "false equality" in which the "proper vocation" and very real needs of women are ignored.[20] Society must grant women the fundamental rights due to *persons,* but it must also respect and provide for their special prerogatives and needs as *women.* The equality to which women have a claim in justice, he writes,

> is not that false equality which would deny the distinctions laid down by the Creator himself and which would be in contradiction with woman's proper role, which is of such capital importance, at the heart of the family as well as within society. Developments in legislation should, on the contrary, be directed to protecting her proper vocation and at the same time recognizing her independence as a person, and her equal rights to participate in cultural, economic, social and political life.[21]

Pope John Paul II reiterates this concern to protect women in their vocation as mothers and to give due recognition to the contribution to society made by their unpaid work in the family. In his encyclical *Laborem exercens (On Human Work),* he calls for

> *a social reevaluation of the mother's role,* of the toil connected with it, and of the need that children have for care, love and affection in order that they may develop into responsible, morally and religiously mature and psychologically stable persons. It will redound to the credit of society to make it possible for a mother—without inhibiting her freedom, without psychological or practical discrimination, and without penalizing her as compared with other women—to devote herself to taking care of her children and educating them in accordance with their needs, which vary with age.[22]

The Pope's admonition is directed not to women but to governments: "Society must be structured in such a way that wives and

---

20. In Church documents, "proper," as in "proper nature," refers to what is distinctive and irreducible, for example, a woman's capacity for motherhood is something that belongs to her "proper" nature.

21. Apostolic letter, *Octogesima adveniens (A Call to Action),* 13 (ND 1760).

22. *Laborem exercens,* 19 (ND 2179).

mothers are *not in practice compelled* to work outside the home." He deplores "the mentality which honors women more for their work outside the home than for their work within the family"[23] and defends a mother's right to devote herself to her family full-time.

Along with this positive promotion of "women's rights," the magisterium condemns legislation that demands for women, as a "right," the option of bearing a child outside of marriage and of aborting a child. The Catholic Church rejects the idea that the equalization of rights requires the identical treatment of women and men.

WOMEN'S EQUAL RIGHTS IN THE CHURCH

This development in Catholic teaching has implications, of course, for the status of women as members of the Church. Conciliar and post-conciliar teaching explicitly encourages women's increased participation in the Church's life and mission, and this has gradually been implemented. This can be seen in the revisions to the Code of Canon Law (1983), the admission of women to the non-ordained ministries, and papal teaching on Christian marriage.

The Second Vatican Council and Post-Conciliar Developments

Baptism, the sacrament of faith, is the foundation of Christian life; it is completed by Confirmation and participation in the mystery of the Eucharist. All believers who receive these sacraments of initiation possess a common dignity and common vocation to holiness. They receive the indwelling Holy Spirit, are incorporated into the body of Christ, and share in the divine nature as adopted children of God. Are baptized women full-fledged members of the Church? Do they have equal rights and dignity with baptized men? In *Lumen gentium* (art. 32), the Council answered "yes" to both questions:

> The chosen People of God is, therefore, one: "one Lord, one faith, one baptism" (Ephesians 4:5); there is a common dignity of members deriving from the rebirth in Christ, a common grace as sons and daughters, a common vocation to perfection, one salvation, one hope and undivided charity. In Christ and in the church there is, then, no inequality arising from race or nationality, social condition or sex.

---

23. *Familiaris consortio (On the Family)*, 23 (ND 2181).

This affirmation is followed by the citation of Galatians 3:28: the new creation in Christ overcomes the social patterns of discrimination that existed between Jew and Greek, slave and free, male and female.[24] According to the Council, "there is neither male nor female" means that baptized women and men have equal status in the Church. Females, who could not be directly initiated into the covenant of Israel through circumcision, are admitted to the New Covenant on an equal basis with males through Baptism. Girls and women are confirmed and admitted to the Eucharist, along with boys and men, in the same ceremonies. All participate, in their own way, in Christ's triple office as priest, prophet, and king. All share in the common priesthood of believers.[25]

In article nine of the decree *Apostolicam actuositatem (On the Apostolate of the Laity)*, the Council specifically mentions that women's advancement in society must have as its counterpart their greater involvement in the Church's mission.[26] Lay women were already exercising leadership in Catholic Action and the lay apostolate before the Council, and they had many opportunities for apostolic witness in the "marketplace." Women religious in congregations of apostolic life already had canonical status and a long tradition of publicly recognized service offered in the name of the Church. Women both lay and religious anticipated, however, that as a result of the Council they would be able to take a larger part in the Church's internal life.

Many apostolic activities were already open to women. Paul VI enumerated them: "religious education and spiritual formation, preparation for the sacraments, overtures to those baptized persons who are almost completely ignorant of the faith, the approach to non-Christians, the acceptance and association with the poor and those on the margins of society, the leadership of Catholic Action, the discernment and fostering of vocations, participation in Catholic

---

24. Van der Meer (p. 42) explains that this formula reverses the Jewish males' daily prayers praising God that he was not a Gentile, a woman, or an ignoramus (later changed to "a slave").

25. *Lumen gentium,* 31; see also 10–11.

26. A more extensive treatment was ultimately reduced to one sentence: "Since in our days women are taking an increasingly active share in the entire life of society, it is very important that their participation in the various sectors of the church's apostolate should likewise develop." See Rose McDermott, *The Legal Condition of Women in the Church: Shifting Policies and Norms* (Washington, D.C.: The Catholic University of America, Canon Law Studies No. 499, 1979), for an account of this.

socio-professional movements."[27] To augment these, the International Study Commission composed a "Questionnaire on the Participation of Women in the Life of the Ecclesial Community" for use by Bishops' Conferences.[28] At its close, the Commission proposed several recommendations, for example, the appointment of competent women to posts in the Departments of the Holy See "whose work calls for their contribution," and a thorough study of women's access to the non-ordained ministries, participation in the liturgy, and capacity to exercise jurisdiction (in the wide sense) within the Church. It requested that the revised Code of Canon Law provide for women's full participation in the life and mission of the Church.[29]

A report on "The Role of Women in Evangelization," prepared for the 1974 Synod of Bishops and issued by the Congregation for the Evangelization of Peoples in 1976, also recognized women's contributions and recommended that they be prepared for and entrusted with expanded responsibilities so that they might be able to "play their full role" and participate in decision making in the Church.[30] The report suggests that Sisters who have taken up duties previously reserved to priests should be commissioned by the bishop in some formal way.

The impact of these and many other recommendations and reports began to be felt in the Church's practice. It was in the revision of the Code of Canon Law,[31] however, that the Council's teaching on baptismal equality was most directly addressed.

The 1983 Code of Canon Law

One of the ten principles adopted to guide the revision of the Church's law was the "fundamental equality of all the members of the Christian faithful."[32] All of the baptized, the *Christifideles*, have a common

---

27. "Women/Balancing Rights and Duties," 552.

28. *The Church and the International Women's Year 1975* (Vatican City: Pontifical Council for the Laity), 105–111 and the *International Women's Year 1975 Study Kit* (Washington, D.C.: USCC, 1975).

29. Ibid., 162, and *Study Kit*, 28–29.

30. See *Origins* 5:44 (April 22, 1976): 702–706.

31. We are limiting our consideration to the Latin Church.

32. McDermott, "Woman, Canon Law On," in *New Catholic Encyclopedia*, second edition.

legal status, without distinction as to sex and before any differentiation into lay and ordained. Canon 208 of the 1983 Code expresses this:

> From their rebirth in Christ, there exists among all the Christian faithful a true equality regarding the dignity and the action by which they all contribute in the building up of the Body of Christ according to each one's own condition and function.[33]

This "true equality" of the baptized has to do with their dignity and activity. It does not preclude a variety of gifts and charisms, services and offices, however, for the canon acknowledges that the baptized "cooperate in the building up of the Body of Christ" in diverse ways. In fact, the preceding canon (207 §1) states clearly that by divine institution some of the Christian faithful are clerics, or "sacred ministers," and others are "lay persons."[34] The phrase "according to each one's own condition and function" provides for the distinctions that are made on the basis of one's "condition," for example, as lay or ordained, consecrated religious, married, and so on. Although no women are among the ordained, they possess a "true equality" with men as members of the Christian faithful.

The improvement in the legal condition of women within the Church is due, in fact, to the Second Vatican Council's teaching on the fundamental equality of the non-ordained[35] with the ordained faithful. For the most part, the new roles open to women after the Council are identical with the new roles open to non-ordained men.

This new understanding had to be put into effect, however, by revising some canons of the 1917 Code that did discriminate against women on the basis of their sex.[36] According to Rose McDermott, there were 33 such canons, and they affect women's rights in Christian marriage, in religious life, and in the non-ordained ministries and other

---

33. Canon 208; see *Lumen gentium*, 32.

34. Canon 207 §1. Canon 207 §2 explains that consecrated religious, drawn from both states, belong to the Church's life and holiness, not its hierarchical structure.

35. "Non-ordained" is used in order to encompass with a single term the laity and consecrated but non-ordained religious. See *Lumen gentium*, 31, where "laity" excludes consecrated religious.

36. The following analysis draws on the work of Rose McDermott, *The Legal Condition of Women* (1979), and Nancy Reynolds, *A Comparison of the Specific Juridic Status of Women in the 1917 and 1983 Codes of Canon Law* (Washington, D.C.: The Catholic University of America, Canon Law Studies, 1984).

ecclesiastical roles. McDermott infers that the discrimination follows from four outdated presuppositions about women's "nature."[37] First, women have a subordinate (or "subject") status vis-à-vis men; thus, they require guidance and direction from men as their wives or social inferiors. Second, women are potential or actual "temptresses"; therefore, the law should protect men, especially clerics, from any feminine presence or behavior that may be the occasion of sin. Third, women are characteristically deficient in intelligence and good judgment, and, therefore, they need male assistance and advice. Fourth, women are typically timid and scrupulous; thus, the law must take care not to burden them. Overall, the law suggests that women are in need of male governance, instruction, and protection both in family life and in their religious congregations, and that they are not capable of participating in ecclesiastical affairs in which lay men should be involved. McDermott finds that these presuppositions, reflected in the standard commentaries, are reinforced by the citation of key New Testament texts relating to women.

According to the 1917 Code, a married woman was unilaterally "subject" to her husband: she was to share his domicile and place of burial, and if he belonged to another rite, she might join it (and their children must do so), but not vice versa. Women religious were also dependent on men. The Code included a significant body of "protective" legislation for female—but not male—religious. Much of it concerns episcopal supervision in matters such as governance, sacramental discipline (especially with respect to the sacrament of Penance), finances and other temporalities, admissions and dismissals, and for some the observance of cloister. Candidates for women's religious congregations had to be examined by clerics as to their freedom and intention prior to profession of vows, and clerics were permitted to excuse women from legal obligations that might provoke scruples.

Some canons protected men against the provocations women might cause: women were to be seated separately at liturgical services, instructed about modest attire, and excluded from the choir, processions, and various church societies. Clerics were to avoid contact with women apart from their assigned duties, and women religious were to travel in pairs outside the convent.

---

37. McDermott, *Legal Condition*, 153–155.

As for questions of precedence, the law generally gave men and boys preference over women and girls in both the reception and the administration of the sacraments. For example, if infants of both sexes were presented for Baptism, the boys would be baptized first, and in an emergency, a man in preference to a woman should administer Baptism. Opportunities open to lay men, such as preparing for and participating in diocesan synods, were not open to women.

By a sympathetic reading, we could view these canons as "paternalistic" more than "patriarchal." In an age when women could not readily attain the same educational standard as men, when they were prohibited from obtaining theological or canonical training and had no direct access to the hierarchy, these canons obliged the men who had these advantages to render them assistance. Not all provisions, however, can be justified on this reading. To some extent the 1917 Code proposed a legal "double standard." In this, it reflects the common assessment of women's status at the time it was drawn up.

The 1983 Code of Canon Law has remedied this situation. As a result of the revision, women now have essentially the same juridical status as men in the Catholic Church. The revision entailed the elimination of discriminatory laws, provision for the admission of non-ordained persons to certain ecclesiastical offices and responsibilities, and the formulation of new canons (for example, concerning membership in diocesan pastoral councils, finance councils, and so on). In fact, non-ordained women and men are now eligible to participate in diocesan synods with consultative vote; to be members of parish and diocesan pastoral councils and finance councils; and to serve as diocesan chancellors, professors of philosophy, theology, and canon law in seminaries, and as judges, promoters of justice, defenders of the bond, and other positions in a Church tribunal. They are able to be appointed to certain other ecclesiastical offices, and may be called on as consultants and expert advisors. They can be deputed, in the case of genuine need and on a temporary basis, to supply certain tasks proper to the ordained such as preaching, administering Baptism, witnessing marriages, and assisting in the care of a parish.

It is clear that the real distinction that remains in canon law is that between the ordained and the non-ordained.[38] Because no women are among the ordained, this distinction is often perceived as a distinction based on sex. But this is a mistake, because most men are not ordained either. The distinction is based, rather, on the fact that "by Christ's will some [granted, these are always men] are appointed teachers, dispensers of the mysteries and pastors for the others."[39]

Nancy Reynolds points out that the situation of women and men is not precisely "equal" in three cases.[40] The first two pertain to a child's place of origin and rite. If there is a doubt about a child's place of origin, it is settled in favor of the mother, and—if the parents belong to different rites and cannot agree—the child's rite is settled in favor of the father. In Reynolds's opinion, these are reasonable solutions and not instances of unjust discrimination. The third exception concerns the lay ministries of lector and acolyte (canon 230 §1). According to the apostolic letter *Ministeria quaedam* of Pope Paul VI (1972), which suppressed the minor orders and established these functions as lay ministries, installation as lector or acolyte is reserved to males by reason of "venerable tradition." Women may be admitted to the exercise of these and other liturgical functions (canon 230 §2) on a temporary basis, but they cannot be permanently installed (or "instituted") in them. Reynolds thinks this can be seen as "a direct carryover from earlier tradition," namely, the tradition of admitting candidates for Holy Orders to the "minor orders" of lector and acolyte as steps on the way toward priestly ordination. Viewed from this perspective, it does not violate the principle of equality to reserve permanent installation in these ministries to men, while deputing women to exercise these functions when necessary.[41]

The Advancement of Women in Liturgical Ministries

The question of whether girls and women may be allowed to function as altar servers is related to this. There was an initial hesitation after

---

38. As Reynolds puts it (p. 54): "There is not a woman-man distinction; there is an ordained–non-ordained distinction."

39. *Lumen gentium*, 32.

40. Reynolds, 53–54.

41. McDermott, "Woman, Canon Law On," regards this, along with the imposition on nuns, but not monks, of papal norms regulating cloister, as discriminatory.

the Council about admitting women to the liturgical functions belonging to the baptized,[42] a hesitation surely due to the long tradition of reserving ministry in the sanctuary to men. When women were first appointed as readers, commentators, and cantors, they were required to stand outside the sanctuary, and several instructions were issued prohibiting women and girls from serving at the altar.

Gradually, however, as the service of extraordinary ministers of Holy Communion was expanded to include administering the chalice at Mass and taking the Eucharist to the sick in hospitals and in their homes, women who exercised this role had occasion to enter the sanctuary and approach the altar. Given this development, it was hard to explain the prohibition of female altar servers. Many advocates of equal rights for women requested that the longstanding tradition be reconsidered.

The question was settled in 1992 by a ruling of the Pontifical Commission for the Interpretation of Legislative Texts.[43] Service at the altar is now counted among those liturgical functions that may be committed to baptized persons by temporary deputation. It is left to the episcopal conferences to determine whether girls and women may function as altar servers. Where the episcopal conference is willing, individual bishops may permit this in their dioceses.[44] The ruling does not specifically authorize female altar servers; it has a permissive and not "preceptive" character, that is, pastors may allow this but they are not under any obligation to do so.

This ruling is significant, despite these qualifications, because it clarifies the principle. In principle, if not in practice, the equal access of women and men to the non-ordained ministries—apart from installation as lector and acolyte—has now been secured. According to Catholic teaching, certain ministerial functions belong exclusively to the ordained; their exercise requires the sacramental "character" imparted at ordination. Other functions are "proper" to the ordained but do not require the character of Holy Orders; these can be

---

42. *Immensae caritatis* (1973) ranked persons according to their "suitability" for liturgical roles: seminarians and male religious, then women religious; lay men, and finally lay women.

43. The Commission replied affirmatively to a *dubium:* "Whether service at the altar can be counted among the liturgical functions that lay persons, either men or women, can fulfill according to canon 230 §2?"

44. See "Use of Female Altar Servers Allowed," *Origins* 23:45 (April 28, 1994): 777.779.

entrusted to the non-ordained faithful, but only for a serious reason and on a temporary basis. The consequences of this have been spelled out in some detail in *Ecclesia de mysterio,* the interdiscasterial *Instruction on Certain Questions regarding the Collaboration of the Non-Ordained Faithful in the Sacred Ministry of the Priest* (1997). According to this instruction, women, as sharers in the common priesthood of the baptized, are capable of being entrusted with the same pastoral functions as non-ordained men. The non-ordained faithful who collaborate with the ordained in their exercise of pastoral care do so on the basis of the sacraments of initiation and—for certain public leadership functions[45]—by reason of a juridical intervention on the part of the hierarchy. Preference in the exercise of liturgical ministries is given to men over women only when those men have been installed in one of the lay ministries or have been ordained deacons, priests, or bishops.

The Equality of the Spouses in Christian Marriage

The 1983 Code of Canon Law effected a change in the status of married women that reflects the Council's teaching on the sacrament of Marriage in *Gaudium et spes* (arts. 48 and 49). Drawing on this source, the new canon defining Marriage refers to "the matrimonial covenant, by which a man and a woman establish between themselves a partnership of the whole of life."[46]

It is necessary to take note of how the magisterium reconciles this egalitarian understanding of marriage with the Pauline teaching on male headship and female subordination. New Testament texts, called the *Haustafeln* or household codes, which admonish wives to be submissive to their husbands (for example, Ephesians 5:21–33; Colossians 3:18–19; 1 Peter 3:1–7) had to be reconsidered.[47] According to the traditional interpretation, the subjection of wives to their husbands followed from the order of creation (1 Corinthians 11:8–10; 1 Timothy 2:13) and also from the punishment imposed on Eve (Genesis 3:16). Even when this hierarchical construal of the relations

---

45. In the United States, some are entrusted to "lay ecclesial ministers."

46. See Can. 1055 § 1 and *Gaudium et spes,* 49.

47. Many Anglican and Protestant theologians had already achieved a scholarly consensus on this question.

between the sexes was benignly interpreted as compatible with the dignity and liberty of the woman,[48] it was still the wife who was "subject," not the husband. Theologians pointed out that both spouses are equal before God, as persons and as baptized Christians; they appealed to 1 Corinthians 7:3 and 11:11–12 to demonstrate that Paul's exhortations to wifely "submission" do not govern the relationship of the spouses in its entirety. But it was Pope John Paul II who directly addressed the question of the wife's subjection to her husband (and women's subjection to men more generally) as raised by the letters in the Pauline corpus. He shows how the "Gospel innovation"—incorporated into the Pauline text on Baptism,[49] Galatians 3:28—has affected the relationship of spouses in Christian marriage, and how Christ's victory overcomes the opposition between the sexes introduced by sin and restores the relationship of man and woman portrayed in the first chapters of Genesis.

Pope John Paul II examines very thoroughly[50] the situation at "the beginning" to which Jesus restores wounded humanity (Matthew 19:4). In his Christian "rereading" of the first three chapters of Genesis, the Pope discerns that man and woman are made in the "image of God" (1:27) not only as individuals but together. As a "communion of persons," in the "one flesh" of married love (Genesis 2:24), man and woman mirror the communion of persons in the Trinity. Their relationship is characterized by equality, mutuality, and reciprocity. The estrangement from God brought about by sin, however, distorts the relationship between the sexes: it is no longer untroubled and free of self-seeking, and women find themselves at a particular disadvantage (Genesis 3:16).[51]

Turning to the New Testament, the Pope sees that Jesus, as depicted in the Gospels, reveals in a particular way the reality of the redemption for women. He is "*a promoter of women's true dignity* and of the *vocation* corresponding to this dignity."[52]

---

48. Pope Pius XI, in *Casti connubii* (*On Christian Marriage*, 1930), 28, defending the family against the liberal feminist views of women's liberation, qualifies this teaching very carefully.

49. Some exegetes regard this as a pre-Pauline text. See Albert Vanhoye, "Church's Practice in Continuity with New Testament Teaching," in *From Inter Insigniores*, 151–157, at 155.

50. His catecheses on the book of Genesis were collected as *Theology of the Body*, 42–51.

51. Ibid., 120–122.

52. *Mulieris dignitatem*, 12. See 12–16 for his reflection on the example of Jesus found in the Gospels.

Jesus' teaching and behavior with respect to women "clearly constitutes an 'innovation' "[53] when compared to the customs of his time. In word and deed, the Lord opposes the tradition that failed to respect the dignity of women and their rightful place in marriage; he calls his hearers back to God's original plan (Matthew 19:4). He is keenly aware that the inheritance of sin includes a "habitual discrimination against women in favor of men,"[54] and he upholds an ethical standard that attacks male domination at its source, namely, in the sinful attitudes that lead to rivalry and the domination of one sex by the other. The "Gospel innovation" promises healing for the wounds sin has inflicted on the relationships between the sexes.

The Pope relates the evidence of this "Gospel innovation" to Saint Paul's assertion that in Christ there is "no male and female" (Galatians 3:28).[55] Saint Paul, he explains, announces the end of the antagonism between the sexes. In the power of Christ's victory, baptized men and women can overcome fear and concupiscence and live together in mutual respect and harmony. This baptismal text, then, becomes the key for understanding the relationship of spouses in Christian marriage.

With this key, the Pope proposes a rereading of the "great analogy" in Ephesians 5.[56] According to this text, the relation between husband and wife illuminates that between Christ and the Church, and vice versa. Used as the first lesson for the nuptial Mass since the sixteenth century, the reading from Ephesians customarily began with verse 22: "Wives, be subject to your husbands as the Church is to Christ. For the husband is the head of the wife." The "subjection" appears to be only on the part of the wife—unilateral.

The Pope's meditation on this text begins, instead, with the verse in which husbands are admonished to love their wives just as Christ loved the Church and gave himself up for her (verse 25). Love, the "sincere gift of self," must replace domination on the husband's part. His "headship," like Christ's, must be exercised by "giving himself

---

53. Ibid., 13.

54. Ibid., 14. The originality of this analysis lies in the rereading of the first three chapters of Genesis, which discovers the complete equality and mutuality of man and woman as God's original design.

55. *Mulieris dignitatem*, 16.

56. Ibid., 24.

up" for his wife.[57] For the Pope, the whole exhortation to the spouses, read in the light of the "Gospel innovation," is governed by verse 21: "Be subject to one another out of reverence for Christ." If wives are to be subject to their husbands (which they are), husbands are likewise to be subject to their wives.[58] From his analysis of this passage the Pope concludes that "whereas in the relationship between Christ and the Church the subjection is only on the part of the Church, in the relationship between husband and wife the 'subjection' is not one-sided but mutual." In Christ, the submission is not unilateral but bilateral.

The Pope recognizes that the apostolic writings sometimes betray a more traditional interpretation of the relationship between the sexes. A footnote (no. 49) lists the texts of the "household codes" and the "Pauline ban." This evidence notwithstanding, he maintains, the "'innovation' of Christ is a fact: it constitutes the unambiguous content of the evangelical message and is the result of the Redemption."[59] Making explicit his intention to interpret this for today, the Pope recalls how long it took to grasp the practical implications in the social order of the equality announced in Galatians 3:28 regarding the condition of "slave and free." Centuries passed before the full impact of this text was felt and slavery abolished. So too "the awareness that in marriage there is a mutual 'subjection of the spouses out of reverence for Christ,' and not just that of the wife to the husband, must gradually establish itself in hearts, consciences, behavior and customs." The Pope repeats a third time this challenge to live according to the ethos of the Redemption: "All the reasons in favor of the 'subjection' of woman to man in marriage must be understood in the sense of a 'mutual subjection' of both 'out of reverence for Christ.'"[60] This applies not just to husbands and wives but to all relations between men and women in the community of the redeemed.

In itself, this affirmation of the equal dignity of husband and wife, and of men and women is hardly surprising, given the many

---

57. Ibid., 24. See Francis Martin, *The Feminist Question: Feminist Theology in the Light of Christian Tradition* (Grand Rapids, Michigan: William B. Eerdmans, 1994), 399–400, for more on male headship.

58. *Mulieris dignitatem*, 24. For more on this, see John S. Grabowski, "Mutual Submission and Trinitarian Self-Giving," *Angelicum* 74:4 (1997): 489–512.

59. *Mulieris dignitatem*, 24.

60. Ibid.

explicit statements of the magisterium cited earlier in this chapter. It is, nevertheless, important as an official exposition of a New Testament text that many Catholics—and many other Christians—continue to regard as problematic.

CONCLUSION

We have seen that there has been a development in Catholic teaching regarding the equality of women with men, with respect to basic human rights, in the social order. This doctrine has also been applied in the Church: today, all of the baptized, the *Christifideles,* without respect to sex, have the same juridic status in canon law. This doctrine has gradually been clarified in official teaching, and it has affected the Church's practice in many ways. We should note, however, that the equality of the baptized has to do with access to salvation, not access to particular offices or vocations. The Church teaches that different vocations and gifts are bestowed by the Holy Spirit; they belong within a single "communion" and complement one another (see 1 Corinthians 12:4–31). The Lord himself has entrusted certain offices to some and not to others. These gifts and offices are not the subject of a "right," but are free gifts given to build up the body of Christ so that all may reach salvation and the attain the holiness of the saints.

Chapter 3

Three Objections to the Church's Teaching

The starting point for the explanation of the Catholic tradition given in *Ordinatio sacerdotalis* is the Church's settled doctrine regarding the origin and nature of the ministerial priesthood. The starting point for advocates of women's ordination, on the other hand, is the Church's contemporary teaching that women have equal rights and equal dignity with men. The first starting point confirms the tradition, whereas the second is commonly thought to call it into question.

In order to understand the debate that has taken place, it is necessary to evaluate three fundamental objections to Catholic teaching. The first, raised by liberal feminists, protests that the Church unjustly denies women equal opportunity and equal rights with men by excluding them from a role of public leadership on the basis of stereotypical views of women as a class. The second, raised by Catholic feminists, especially feminist theologians, adopts the same objection but traces the Church's practice to a flawed theory regarding the nature and value of sexual difference, a "faulty anthropology." The third objection, raised by Protestant Christians who favor women's ordination, asks why women are eligible for Baptism but not for ordination. It rests on the view that the ordained ministry is an office, not a sacrament distinct from Baptism. By taking the measure of these objections, we hope to grasp more deeply the teaching of *Ordinatio sacerdotalis*.

Objection 1: The Exclusion of Women Is Unjust

Given the explicit affirmation of women's equal rights with men in contemporary papal and conciliar teaching, it is understandable that people ask what prevents women from being ordained to the priesthood. Why should this particular "leadership position" constitute an exception? To feminists looking at the Catholic Church from the outside, the exclusion of women from the ordained ministry appears to be unjust and "sexist," a violation of women's equal rights.

The chief goal of the "second wave" of liberal feminism[1] has been to secure for women the fundamental human rights that men enjoy. Feminists are eager to correct social stereotypes that portray women as inferior to and different from men, because these have been used to confine them to the private and domestic sphere, segregated from public life. Feminists challenge as unjust any rule, regulation, or custom that excludes women and girls, solely on the grounds of their sex, from any occupation or institution open to men and boys. They have coined the term "sexism," a counterpart to "racism," to name the injustice that arises from the belief that one sex is superior to the other, and that finds expression in formal and informal social patterns of differential treatment.

To counter reliance on stereotypes and on an exclusive attention to the "difference" between the sexes, liberal feminists of the 1970s placed an almost exclusive emphasis on "sameness."[2] They consciously adopted the "civil rights" analogy, that is, they compared the situation of women to that of African American citizens who were denied their civil rights under the law and effectively barred from various realms of public life on the basis of harmful racial stereotypes. The feminist strategy for gaining equal access to employment and higher education and for promoting "affirmative action" on behalf of women involved insisting on the "sameness" of the sexes. In 1970, an amendment to the Constitution, the Equal Rights Amendment (ERA), was proposed to Congress. It read: "Equality of rights under the

---

1 The "second wave" is usually dated as beginning in the 1960s.

2. It is widely agreed that this constitutes the chief difficulty in feminist theory. See Schneiders, *Beyond Patching*, 10–11.

law shall not be denied or abridged by the United States or by any State on account of sex." This amendment would have rendered unconstitutional any law that granted one sex different rights than the other.[3]

One can readily understand how, in the context of this struggle and on the understanding that the priesthood is essentially a role of public leadership, many regarded gaining access to the ordained ministry as a "justice issue." Barring women as a class from ordination and thus from "equal opportunity" to attain a position that involves the exercise of authority appeared to be based simply on stereotypical thinking concerning the character traits and native capacities of the female sex. Because it is evident that many women are competent to carry out the functions of ordained ministers, and not evident why the Church will not authorize their ordination, the refusal is chalked up to clerical "sexism."

From this perspective, admission to the ordained ministry looks like a question of justice for women, rooted in human rights, even civil rights. Women of demonstrated competence who are barred from positions of public leadership solely on the basis of their sex are said to hit the "stained-glass ceiling" of sex discrimination in the Church. Feminists put the burden of proof on the Church to defend her practice, and they demand an explanation that makes sense within their frame of reference.

Reply 1. No One Has a Right to Priestly Ordination

Being excluded from priestly ordination would constitute an injustice only if women (and men who were not called to or not accepted for Holy Orders) were prevented thereby from attaining some personal advantage that would enhance their ability to achieve the goal of Christian life.[4] Holy Orders, however, is conferred not for "the honor or advantage or benefit of the recipient, but for the service of God and the Church."[5] It is a sacrament "in the service of communion,"[6] that

---

3. The campaign to adopt this amendment failed after repeated efforts to get the necessary number of state ratifications.

4. Women would suffer an injustice, for example, if they were not allowed to be confirmed or to receive the Eucharist.

5. *Inter insigniores*, 6.

6. *Catechism of the Catholic Church*, part two, section two, chapter three.

is, it is ordered to the service of others, and the grace it gives is for the worthy accomplishment of that service.

From the perspective of Catholic doctrine, the priesthood is not a "leadership role" gained on the basis of one's own efforts and accomplishments (John 15:16; see Hebrews 5:4). As *Inter insigniores* teaches,

> the priesthood does not form part of the rights of the individual, but stems from the economy of the mystery of Christ and the Church. The priestly office cannot become the goal of social advancement; no merely human progress of society or of the individual can of itself give access to it: it is of another order.[7]

The feminist objection is rooted in the supposition that the priesthood and the episcopate represent the pinnacle of achievement for the members of the Catholic Church. Those who are prevented from achieving this status are thought to be deprived of access to a station that might in some way be their due. But this is not the case. The priesthood is not a "career." The priest is ordained not for his personal advantage, but to serve the rest of the baptized in their quest for salvation and holiness by providing them with Christ's gifts in word and sacrament.

In any case, all are called to holiness, without respect to sex, age, ethnicity, or any other social condition. "The greatest in the Kingdom of Heaven are not the ministers but the saints."[8] From this perspective, there is no injustice in the fact that some are called to Holy Orders and others are not. Pope John Paul II underlines this point when he recalls the unique dignity of the Blessed Virgin Mary and the witness of other eminent women saints. The "hierarchical priesthood" is placed, he reminds us, at the service of the "hierarchy of holiness," where "to reign is to serve."[9]

The major flaw in this feminist objection is its assumption that the Church is organized on the principles of a democratic society, indeed, that the Church is essentially a voluntary society of Christian believers who are responsible for creating and maintaining an institutional order that serves its purposes. But, as *Inter insigniores* (art. 6) asserts,

---

7. *Inter insigniores*, 6.

8. *Inter insigniores*, 6; see also CCC § 1578.

9. See *Mulieris dignitatem*, 5 and 27; *Ordinatio sacerdotalis*, 3.

one must note the extent to which the Church is a society different from other societies, original in her nature and in her structures. . . . The pastoral charge . . . is not a simple government, comparable to the modes of authority found in States. It is not granted by people's spontaneous choice: even when it involves designation through election, it is the laying on of hands and the prayer of the successors of the apostles that guarantee God's choice.

Notwithstanding the fact that baptized members of the Church legitimately claim the right to participate in her life, no one among them, according to Catholic teaching, has the right to be ordained: "to consider the ministerial priesthood as a human right would be to misjudge its nature completely."[10]

Reply 2. Women Have Access to Leadership in the Church

Priests are not the only ones who hold public leadership roles in the Church. As we have seen, the 1983 Code of Canon Law opens many new opportunities for service to qualified men and women. They are not ordained, but rather fulfill these offices on the basis of the sacraments of initiation and, for some, of the sacrament of Marriage.[11] Women, as members of the Christian faithful, have acquired new opportunities to exercise leadership; they have access to virtually the same roles as non-ordained men, and on the same basis.[12]

Women can share in decision making by taking part in parish and diocesan pastoral councils, diocesan synods, and commissions of various kinds.[13] They can qualify for full-time positions in the parish, the diocese, and Catholic institutions by acquiring theological, ministerial, and other professional training.[14] They can participate not only as volunteers and subordinates but also as professionals, collaborators, and leaders; not only on parish staffs but in middle management

---

10. Ibid. See Benedict Ashley, *Justice in the Church: Gender and Participation* (Washington, D.C.: The Catholic University of America Press, 1996) for more on the rights of the baptized.

11. See CCC, §§ 901–912.

12. We have described many of these in chapter two.

13. See *Christifideles laici*, 50–51 (ND 1785).

14. An important factor since the Second Vatican Council has been the admission of women to degree programs for the advanced study of theology, scripture, canon law, and church administration. St. Mary's College in Notre Dame, Indiana, had opened a doctoral degree in theology to women in 1943, but this was an exception.

and executive positions. Women have been pioneers in "lay ecclesial ministry," that is, in roles of public leadership in the Church that involve close collaboration with the clergy and formal ecclesial recognition.[15] In addition, many women are involved in renewal and "ecclesial" movements or have affiliated with religious congregations; through these associations they can exercise public leadership in service of a specific mission. It should not be forgotten, moreover, that many women religious have long held professional credentials—as educators, medical professionals, and social workers—and have served the Church through the corporate works sponsored or undertaken by their congregations.

It is true, of course, that whereas women are restricted to roles open to the non-ordained, men, provided they meet certain conditions, may also aspire to the "public leadership roles" proper to the ordained. But no one has a "right" to ordination, in such a way that being denied it constitutes an injustice, and no injustice is suffered by those who are not admitted to the priesthood.

OBJECTION 2: EXCLUSION IS BASED ON A "FAULTY ANTHROPOLOGY"

Catholic feminists, in particular feminist theologians,[16] also regard women's exclusion from priestly ordination as unjust. They suspect that women are excluded on the basis of a "faulty anthropology," and their suspicion is not entirely baseless, for the theological rationale offered in the past was deficient on this score. In light of this, and of their reading of the "theological arguments" proposed in *Inter insigniores* (art. 5), these theologians charge that the Church excludes women from the priesthood on the basis of an outmoded, dualistic anthropology that gives unwarranted importance to the difference

---

15. See Zeni Fox, *New Ecclesial Ministry: Lay Professionals Serving the Church* (Franklin, Wisconsin: Sheed and Ward, 2002) and *Women and Jurisdiction: An Unfolding Reality—The LCWR Study of Selected Church Leadership Roles,* ed. Anne Munley, et al (Silver Spring, Maryland: Leadership Conference of Women Religious, 2002).

16. "Feminist theologians" take the "full flourishing of women" as the norm for theological reflection. They believe that women's "flourishing" must include the possibility of being ordained. Not all women theologians are "feminist" theologians in this sense (some are called "papal feminists"), and not all feminist theologians are women.

between the sexes.[17] These critics object that the magisterium's appeal to the maleness of Christ and to the nuptial symbolism that it favors relies on a flawed theory of sexual complementarity.

Feminist theologian Elizabeth A. Johnson articulates this position as follows: "Many who read John Paul II's endorsement of women's equality with men as image of God wonder why it does not lead him to posit equality in all ministries of church life and governance." She then explains that "the reason is that he is still using the traditional dualistic view that men and women embody human nature in two contrasting ways, which means that they each possess special characteristics, which means that they must play distinct social roles."[18] Johnson characterizes the Pope's "model" of sexual complementarity as follows:

> "Masculine nature" with its active orientation to rationality, order, and decision making is equipped for leadership in the public realm. "Feminine nature" with its receptive orientation to love, life, and nurturing is fit for the private domain of childbearing, homemaking, and care for the vulnerable.

Elizabeth Johnson acknowledges that real progress has been made in recent papal teaching within this "dualistic masculine-feminine framework," but she questions whether the framework itself does not impose undue limitations on women. In her view, it is the Pope's conviction that there are "essential differences between masculine and feminine versions of human nature" that prevents him from applying his teaching on the equality of men and women to Holy Orders. It is by reason of his dualistic or "binary" model of theological anthropology[19] that Pope John Paul II "justifies the practice of excluding women from positions of ritual leadership and public governance."[20]

---

17. See Catherine Mowry LaCugna's influential article, "Catholic Women as Ministers and Theologians," *America* 167:10 (October 10, 1992): 238–248.

18. "Imaging God, Embodying Christ: Women as a Sign of the Times," in *The Church Women Want*, ed. Elizabeth A. Johnson (New York: Crossroad, 2002): 45–59, at 52.

19. In a "dualistic" or "binary" model, women and men are cast as polar opposites, according to Johnson.

20. "Imaging God," 53. See my essay, "Embodiment: Women and Men, Equal and Complementary," in *The Church Women Want*, 35–44, for a different perspective on papal teaching.

Reply 1. The Ministerial Priesthood Is Not Just a Leadership Role

We have already shown that Pope John Paul II encourages women to participate in public life and to assume leadership, including leadership in the Church's life and mission. Is it likely, then, that he explains the reservation of "positions of ritual leadership and public governance" (that is, the priesthood) to men on the basis of a faulty theory of complementarity? If this were the case, consistency would require him to object to women's participation in other public leadership roles. But he clearly does not object to this. In fact, what is at stake is not simply a "social role," but a sacrament of the apostolic ministry in which those who are ordained function as "signs" of Christ. And the reason the magisterium supplies for reserving it to men is that this represents Christ's will and the Church has no authority to change it.

Reply 2. The Magisterium's Judgment Is Not Based on a Theory of Christian Anthropology

What accounts for the persistent conviction of feminist theologians— in the face of explicit denials—that that the Church prohibits the priestly ordination of women on the grounds that they are not suited for "social roles" of public leadership? The reason is that until quite recently Catholic theologians generally *did* explain the Church's practice, at least in part, by appealing to the difference and the "hierarchical" ordering of the sexes. They appealed as well to the Pauline texts that prohibited women's public teaching in the Church and their exercise of authority over men (1 Corinthians 14:34; 1 Timothy 2:12). Standing behind these, moreover, were other New Testament texts that implied that women were not made in the divine image (1 Corinthians 11:7) and that they were "subject" to men as a consequence of the Fall (1 Timothy 2:13–14).

Many Catholic theologians relied on the teaching of Saint Thomas Aquinas. Thomas asks, "Whether the female sex is an impediment to receiving Orders?" and answers that it is.[21] He offers

---

21. See his commentary on the *Sentences* of Peter Lombard (*In IV Sent.*, dist. 25, q. 2, art. 1., quaestiuncula la, corp.). After his death, one of Saint Thomas's disciples pulled this material together and published it as Question 39 in the *Supplement* to the *Summa Theologiae*.

as scriptural proof the text of 1 Timothy 2:12, combined with a phrase from 1 Corinthians 14:34: "I suffer not a woman to teach [in the Church], nor to use authority over the man."[22] His theological explanation indicates that the male sex is essential not only for the liceity, but also for the validity of ordination, for "since a sacrament is a sign, not only the thing [res], but the signification of the thing, is required." What disqualifies a woman, he reasoned, is that she is in the state of subjection, and thus cannot signify "eminence of degree," a signification essential to the sacrament. Thomas does not actually complete the argument, but scholars presume that the "eminence" to be signified is that of Christ as Head of the Church.

Because the contemporary magisterium has abandoned the view that women are unilaterally subject to men, it obviously does not supply this as the reason women cannot be priests. Because feminist theologians generally take the doctrine of Christian anthropology as their starting point, however, they continue to assume that the Church's judgment has its source in some perceived incapacity or unsuitability on the part of women. Today, Catholic feminists suspect that even if women's exclusion is no longer justified on the grounds that they are *inferior* to men, it is justified on the grounds that they are *different* from men in ways that imply their unsuitability for public leadership.

Undoubtedly, how one construes the difference between the sexes, and how much importance one accords this difference, enters into speculation as to *why* the Lord chose men and not women. But it is imperative to grasp that this is not at the root of the magisterium's judgment. The complementarity of the sexes does not appear among the "fundamental reasons" given for the Church's tradition. It is alluded to in *Ordinatio sacerdotalis,* and it enters into the theological reasoning proposed by *Inter insigniores* to explain the Lord's choice, but in neither document is it given as the reason for the tradition.[23]

---

22. This conflation is found in the canonical texts of the time and suggests Thomas's reliance on that tradition. Theologians used the canonical collections as theological sources, especially in questions pertaining to the sacraments. Thomas would have used the *Glossa Ordinaria* by John Teutonicus, a text commenting on the *Decretum* of Gratian.

23. Joseph Ratzinger confirms that John Paul II limited himself to stating the "fundamental reasons" in *Ordinatio sacerdotalis.* See his introduction to *From "Inter Insigniores,"* 9.

Reply 3. The Magisterium's Judgment Is Grounded in the "Fact" of Jesus' Example

The magisterium does not claim to deduce who is or is not eligible for admission to the priesthood from its understanding of the difference between the sexes. It claims, rather, that this determination was made by the Lord, and that his intention is known from an unbroken tradition of practice that is traced back to his choice of twelve men. Some conception of sexual complementarity plays a part, of course, in discovering *why* the Lord Jesus chose only men to belong to the Twelve, and we will explore that question later. The point to be made here is that the magisterium relies first of all on a tradition that interprets a *fact* of sacred history. It does not rely on a "theory" of complementarity, or even on the biblical doctrine of the creation of the human person as male and female, in making the judgment that priestly ordination is reserved to men.

As has been noted, many people were taken off guard by the reasons Pope Paul VI supplied to the Archbishop of Canterbury. They were not prepared for the line of argument presented in *Inter insigniores*. If they took note of the distinction it drew between "fundamental reasons" and "theological arguments," many—including many theologians—did not attend to its significance. Feminist theologians consistently direct their attention to the "theological arguments" concerning the maleness of Christ and the meaning of sexual complementarity, while disregarding the "fundamental reasons" that appeal to the institution of the priesthood. But the "theological arguments" are proposed only in order to elucidate the "fundamental reasons" for the Church's practice, not to demonstrate—independently—why things must be ordered in this way.

According to a classic principle of interpretation in Catholic theology, when the magisterium affirms a divinely revealed truth, its judgment bears on the precise object of the definition. It relies on the testimony of the scripture, the tradition, and the prior teaching of the Church, not on the motives or arguments from "fittingness" advanced to help explain it. For example, the definition of the Immaculate Conception does not include in its object the speculative explanation advanced by Blessed John Duns Scotus. The principle by which such a distinction may be drawn is not new, but its potential for clarifying this question does not seem to have been recognized until the 1970s.

As Catholic theologians reexamined the biblical and patristic evidence for the Church's practice and the explanations offered in its support by the Scholastics, they recognized that some of the reasons put forward in the past had to be rejected because they entailed historically and culturally conditioned presuppositions about the inferiority of women and their "subject status."[24] Some scholars observed, however, that the reasons which had to be abandoned were actually "theological arguments," put forward to explain the doctrinal affirmation, not the "fundamental reasons." They looked beyond the Pauline texts and found evidence of Jesus' will for the priesthood in his way of acting.

As the sifting and testing of evidence proceeded, some theologians, like Haye van der Meer and Karl Rahner, speculated that without these "theological arguments" there was no longer a reason to reserve priestly ordination to men.[25] Others, like Jean Galot and Yves M. J. Congar,[26] proposed that the doctrine actually depended not on these outdated arguments but rather on a "fact," namely, the example of Christ and the apostles that had been maintained in the Church's unbroken tradition of sacramental practice. Thus, two different interpretations of the evidence were advanced by theologians. The magisterium eventually adopted the second interpretation.

It is clear that there is no "saying" of the Lord in the Gospels that indicates his will with respect to women's participation in or exclusion from the apostolic ministry. When the tradition was challenged in the first few centuries, some Fathers and theologians defended it by turning to the letters of Saint Paul and citing passages about women's conduct in the Church (the "Pauline ban") or their

---

24. This is acknowledged in *Inter insigniores*, 1.

25. Haye Van der Meer, *Women Priests*, and Karl Rahner, "Women and the Priesthood," in *Concern for the Church* (New York: Crossroad, 1981): 35–47.

26. See Jean Galot, *Mission et ministère de la femme* (Paris: Lethielleux, 1973), and Yves M. J. Congar, "Simples Réflexions," *Vie Consacrées* 44 (1972): 310–314, and "Bulletin de Théologie: Les ministères—Les femmes et les ministères ordonnés," *Revue des sciences philsophiques et théologiques* 58 (October 1974): 638–642. Richard Beauchesne, "Scriptural/Theological Argument against Women's Ordination (Simply Stated) and Responses," *Journal of Ecumenical Studies* 32:1 (Winter 1995): 107–113, supplies these references to Congar's views. This "fact" had been discovered in Swedish Lutheran debate. See Stendahl, 19.

status vis-à-vis men.[27] Others, however, scrutinized the Gospels and appealed to Jesus' deeds, that is, to his example in choosing only men as apostles.[28]

Jean Galot noticed the importance for this question of Jesus' novel way of relating to women, given the religious and cultural context of his time.[29] The Lord's evident freedom with respect to these religious and cultural constraints led Galot to conclude that his choice of men and not women for the apostolic ministry was deliberate. Congar, reviewing Galot's work, concurred with his judgment that Jesus' example itself constitutes a "fact." For Congar, while "theological arguments" like the one based on nuptial symbolism may offer valuable insight into the meaning of the tradition, they do not provide the foundation for it. The *fact*, on the other hand, does.[30]

The fact that Jesus did not choose any women to belong to the Twelve, and that the apostles followed his example by handing on the apostolic charge only to men, was seen to be the "fundamental reason." In Congar's opinion, even on the hypothesis that the Lord's choice of men and not women was historically and sociologically conditioned, it is impossible to prove that this was the case.[31] This supposition would be simply an argument from silence. Ultimately, *Inter insigniores* concurs with this:

> No one however has ever proved—*and it is clearly impossible to prove*—that [Jesus'] attitude is inspired only by social and cultural reasons. As we have seen, an examination of the Gospels shows on the contrary that Jesus broke with the prejudices of his time, by widely contravening the discriminations practiced with regard to women. One therefore cannot

---

27. The absence of a dominical "saying" may have prompted the use of the Pauline passages. See Simon Francis Gaine, "Ordination to the Priesthood: 'That the one who acts in the person of Christ the Head must needs be male but need not be a Jew,'" *New Blackfriars* 83:975 (May 2002): 212–231, at 216.

28. According to *Dei verbum (Dogmatic Constitution on Divine Revelation)*, 7, the apostles handed on what they learned from Jesus' deeds as well as from his spoken words. Deeds and words have an inner unity (*Dei verbum*, 2).

29. Many other scholars had already retrieved this evidence.

30. The magisterium has reclassified Saint Paul's explanations as "theological arguments."

31. "Bulletin de Théologie," 641–642.

maintain that, by not calling women to enter the group of the Apostles, Jesus was simply letting himself be guided by reasons of expediency.[32]

By identifying Jesus' way of acting as the "fact" at the origin of the tradition, theologians like Galot and Congar showed that abandoning the unacceptable arguments once used to explain the Church's tradition did not require abandoning the tradition itself. It rested on a firm foundation. The Commentary released with *Inter insigniores* recalls the principle of interpretation mentioned above: it is "well known that in solemn teaching infallibility affects the doctrinal affirmation, not the arguments intended to explain it."[33] Relying on this principle, the declaration sets aside certain classical arguments and puts forward other less familiar ones to illustrate the meaningfulness of Christ's choice. It states explicitly, however, that the authority of the magisterium is attached not to these "theological arguments,"[34] but only to the "fundamental reasons."

Undoubtedly, some protagonists of the ordination of women, while they take note of the distinction between the data of revelation and theological considerations put forth to elucidate them, still reject the magisterium's case. Insofar as they call into question the "fundamental reasons" themselves, the distinction between reasons and arguments serves no purpose for them. To understand the force of the magisterium's case, however, it is necessary to discover how this distinction works and to notice that it is left to theologians to evaluate the "theological arguments" that have been proposed and to refine and improve on them.[35]

Objection 3: If Women Can Be Baptized, They Can Be Ordained

Members of many other Christian communities question the Catholic tradition of reserving ordination to men on the grounds that Baptism

---

32. Article 4, emphasis added. The passage continues: "For all the more reason, social and cultural conditioning did not hold back the Apostles working in the Greek milieu, where the same forms of discrimination did not exist."

33. *Commentary*, in *From Inter Insigniores*, 70.

34. "In the declaration a very clear distinction will be seen between the document's affirmation of the datum . . . and the theological reflection that then follows." *Commentary*, 69 ff.

35. Ratzinger, "Introduction," 9–10.

establishes a radical equality in Christ. They argue that qualified women should be admitted to ordination not because the Church must conform to society's expectations, but on New Testament principles, as formulated in Galatians 3:28. They ask whether the Catholic Church does not fail to implement her own teaching on the baptismal equality of women with men.

Heirs of the Reformation who are satisfied that the New Testament supports women's equality with men in marriage, public life, and the Church, see no obstacle to their ordination. The eminent New Testament scholar Krister Stendahl, a Lutheran, expressed their conviction this way: "If [women's] emancipation is right, then there is no valid 'biblical' reason not to ordain women."[36] Stendahl's next sentence reveals, however, that this conclusion is based on a Protestant understanding of the ordained ministry: "Ordination cannot be treated as a 'special' problem, since there is no indication that the New Testament sees it as such."[37]

According to the Reformers, the priesthood of the New Testament belongs either to the Lord Jesus (see Hebrews 5:10) or to the Christian community as a whole (see 1 Peter 2:5,9; Revelation 1:6; 5:9–10). As the high priest of the new and eternal covenant, Jesus offered the "once-for-all" sacrifice of the cross. As a "holy priesthood," the baptized offer to God the "spiritual sacrifices" of praise and righteous living. But nowhere in the New Testament are the apostles and their coworkers identified as "priests."[38] On these grounds, the Reformers denied that Christ instituted a ministerial priesthood capable of mediating his own priestly service to the rest of the baptized. In other words, they denied that Holy Orders is a sacrament, instituted by Christ, which confers the grace of the Holy Spirit, and marks the ordained with an indelible spiritual character that bestows on him the sacred power *(sacra potestas)* to offer the sacrifice of the Mass and to forgive sins.

The Protestant Reformers recognized that Christ instituted a ministry of word and sacrament (Baptism and the Lord's Supper),

---

36. Stendahl, 41.

37. Ibid. He also writes (p. 39): "It seems to me impossible to assent . . . to the political emancipation of women while arguing on biblical grounds against ordination of women."

38. That is, the Greek word for priest *(hiereus)* is not used to describe them.

but regarded the ordination that entrusts a person with this ministry as a rite instituted by the Church. This rite of a laying on of hands and invocation of the Holy Spirit sets some of the baptized apart to offer the "special ministry" of word and sacrament to the rest. The ordained are "office-bearers," and in their public office they represent and express the priesthood of the baptized. The sacramental basis of their ministry, in other words, is Baptism. Given this understanding of the ordained ministry, any baptized person—woman or man— should be eligible to seek ordination. Because the Church is comprised of both women and men, both women and men are able to represent it.

Reply 1. Catholic and Protestant Doctrines of Ordination Differ

In recent decades, partners in ecumenical dialogue have given serious reconsideration to this classical Reformation doctrine. Several important consensus statements, in fact, give promise of closing the gap between Protestant, Anglican, Orthodox, and Catholic understandings of the ordained ministry.[39] The unwarranted optimism of some Catholic theologians, however, has serious consequences for our topic.[40] Those who fail to acknowledge the remaining doctrinal differences place the whole burden of explaining the Catholic position on the doctrine of Christian anthropology, that is, on the "theological arguments."

In fact, doctrinal differences about ministry have not been fully resolved.[41] In fact, many Protestant Churches had admitted women to the ordained ministry before these statements of convergence were formulated, and had done so largely on the basis of the classical view we have just sketched out. If ordination is not thought to be a sacrament, if it is not thought to have been instituted by Christ, if it is not believed to "hand on the office entrusted by Christ to his Apostles of teaching, sanctifying, and governing the faithful," then there are no reasons left to prohibit the ordination of women.

---

39. See especially the consensus on Ministry in the Faith and Order Paper, 111, *Baptism, Eucharist and Ministry* (Geneva: World Council of Churches, 1982).

40. See Avery Dulles, "Ecumenism without Illusions: A Catholic Perspective," *First Things* No. 4 (June/July 1990): 20–25, at 22, regarding "hidden disagreements within the previous agreements."

41. See the responses on "Ministry" in *Churches Respond to BEM*, ed. Max Thurian, volumes 1–6 (Geneva: World Council of Churches, 1986–1988, and Chapter III, D, of *The Nature and Purpose of the Church*, Faith and Order Paper 181 (Geneva: World Council of Churches, 1998).

Many Catholic advocates of women's ordination rely heavily on arguments advanced in other Christian churches. Some fail to take note of the difference between the Protestant concept of ordained ministry and the Catholic doctrine of the priesthood. Others notice the difference but minimize it and give credence to the speculative proposals of Catholic theologians who favor the Reformation critique and call into question the Church's settled doctrine of the priesthood.[42] They build a case in favor of women's ordination on the basis of these speculative proposals, even when these proposals have been formally rejected by the magisterium. To understand *Ordinatio sacerdotalis* correctly, it is necessary to appreciate that it takes the settled Catholic doctrine of Holy Orders as its starting point.

Reply 2. Baptismal Equality Pertains to Salvation

Pope John Paul II taught that the baptismal formula quoted by Saint Paul in Galatians 3:28 corresponds, more clearly than some other Pauline texts, to the "Gospel innovation" revealed in Jesus' way of acting with respect to women. For many Protestants, this text supports the ordination of women. For Catholics, however, the equality of the baptized announced by Paul has to do with access to salvation. It has no implications for admission to particular offices or ministries within the Church.[43] We have already examined this from the perspective of canon law. Here, we look at it in terms of the common and the ministerial priesthood.

The high dignity of those sealed with Baptism, confirmed by the Holy Spirit, and nourished at the table of Christ's body and blood is the dignity of the "common priesthood," or the priesthood of the baptized. Through his sacrifice, Jesus has made *all* of his disciples priests of his new and eternal covenant. The priestly people "receives from him a real ontological share in his one eternal priesthood."[44] In Catholic doctrine, the common priesthood is just that—"common"

---

42. For an account of such proposals see Daniel Donovan, *What Are They Saying about the Ministerial Priesthood* (New York: Paulist Press, 1992) and Patrick J. Dunn, *A Re-examination of the Roman Catholic Theology of the Presbyterate* (New York: Alba House, 1990).

43. *Inter insigniores*, 6.

44. Pope John Paul II, Post-Synodal Apostolic Reflection *Pastores dabo vobis (I Will Give You Shepherds)*, 13.

to all the Christian faithful. In other words, it is not "the priesthood of the *laity*," but rather "the priesthood of the *baptized*," regardless of their "condition" or "state of life." It includes not only the lay faithful but also consecrated religious and the clergy. By reason of their baptismal vocation, all of the Christian faithful have the same high dignity and destiny. No one in this company of believers has "second class" status.

But "equality is in no way identity, for the Church is an internally-differentiated body."[45] In the communion of the Church there are many spiritual gifts and diverse vocations. These do not derogate from the equality of the baptized, nor should they be the occasion of jealousy. Rather, the various charisms and callings are given by the Holy Spirit, as Saint Paul said, to build up the body in love (see 1 Corinthians 12:4—13:13).

Reply 3. The Ministerial Priesthood Differs in Kind from the Common Priesthood

The Church's teaching on the equality of all the baptized, affirmed by the Second Vatican Council and consolidated in the 1983 Code of Canon Law, has been repeated in many official documents. Pope John Paul II urged that it be translated into practice,[46] and in many places significant changes have already taken place. Translating the teaching on baptismal equality into practice, however, does not mean admitting women to the Catholic priesthood. Baptismal equality has to do with the exercise of the common priesthood, whereas—according to *Lumen gentium* (art. 10)—the ministerial priesthood is a distinct gift, different "essentially and not only in degree" *(essentia, non gradu tantum)* from the common priesthood.[47]

"Difference in kind" is contrasted with "difference in degree." A difference in "degree" suggests the fuller or more intense possession of something that is common to all, in this case, the grace of Baptism. If the ministerial priesthood differed from the common priesthood

---

45. *Inter insigniores*, 6.

46. See *Christifideles laici*, 51: "the *acknowledgment in theory* of the active and responsible presence of woman in the Church must be *realized in practice*."

47. *Lumen gentium* employs the expression Pius XII used in *Magnificate Dominum* (*The Pope Speaks*, 1:4 [1954]), 378.

only in "degree," it would suggest that the ordained differ from
the non-ordained as the "virtuoso" Catholic differs from the "average"
Catholic. All hope that candidates for ordination are exemplary
Christians, but their ordination does not confer the "fullness" of Baptism.

The ministerial priesthood is different "in kind" or in
"essence" from the common priesthood. Priestly ordination does not
confer "more" of the same grace given in Baptism, leaving the other
baptized somehow shortchanged. "Difference in kind" means that
Holy Orders confers an additional vocational gift. The man ordained
to the ministerial priesthood is consecrated and entrusted with a
distinctive mission. He receives the "sacred power" to carry it out and
the grace to do so worthily, in service to the rest of the baptized.

Ordinatio sacerdotalis (art. 2) says of the apostles: "these twelve
men were not simply given a function which any member of the
Church might later fulfill. Rather, they were drawn into a specific and
intimate association with Christ; they were given the 'mission of
representing Christ the Lord and Redeemer.'" Similarly, Christ calls
the ordained from among the baptized to offer his ministry to the rest,
by his power and his authority. Their ministry is offered not on the
basis of the sacraments of initiation, but on the basis of the sacrament
of Holy Orders. No injustice is suffered by women—or men—who
do not receive this call.

It would be difficult, in fact, to imagine a dignity and destiny
more exalted than that possessed by every Christian. What all the
baptized should aspire to is the "unfolding of baptismal grace"
that belongs to the common priesthood. "Full" participation, for all,
will mean following the Lord Jesus with generous hearts, freely
responding to the impulses of the Holy Spirit, and seeking only to do
God's will. All will be ready even to lose their lives for Christ's sake
(see Luke 9:24).

CONCLUSION

In reply to the liberal feminist objection that women are unjustly
prohibited from access to public leadership roles in the Church, we
assert that the priesthood is not the only form of "public leadership" in
the Catholic Church. Moreover, the priesthood itself is not simply
a "leadership position." It cannot be claimed by any baptized believer

as a right. Rather, this office belongs to the economy of salvation and the Lord freely entrusts it to those whom he chooses.

In reply to the objection of Catholic feminist theologians that the Church unjustly excludes women from priestly ordination on the basis of a faulty anthropology, we insist that the Church does not defend her practice on the basis of an argument from sexual complementarity. She appeals, rather, to the tradition itself, to the fact that Jesus chose only men to belong to the Twelve, and to the witness of the apostolic Church. The feminist objection, then, fails to engage the principal assertion of the magisterium. It confuses the "theological arguments" with the "fundamental reasons."

In reply to the Protestant objection that Catholic practice runs counter to the radical equality established by Baptism, we point out that this objection follows from a Protestant doctrine of ordained ministry, but it does not follow from the Catholic doctrine of the priesthood. According to the Protestant doctrine, the reservation of ordained ministry to men would be unjust because the ordained ministry represents the priesthood of the baptized. The Catholic Church agrees that baptized men and women are equally incorporated into the common priesthood, but teaches that the ministerial priesthood is a distinct vocation to which the Lord calls certain men, for the service of the common priesthood. Therefore, the Church does not regard the exclusion of all women and most men from the ministerial priesthood as unjust.

Chapter 4

The Church's Fundamental Reasons

We have tried to clear the way for the consideration of the Church's teaching by anticipating three objections. We will proceed, now, on the assumption that in the Catholic Church the question of women's ordination is not properly a "justice issue," that the "fundamental reason" given for the tradition is not an appeal to a theory regarding the complementarity of the sexes, and that the equality of women with men in the common priesthood of the baptized does not imply their right to be ordained to the ministerial priesthood.

This chapter will set out, step by step, the "fundamental reasons" given by the magisterium, following in a general way the order adopted by *Inter insigniores*. As we have seen, two competing accounts of the tradition dominated the intra-Catholic debate in the years just prior to the 1976 declaration. One account traces the unbroken tradition of practice back to Christ himself, and to his will for the priesthood expressed in choosing only men as his apostles. The magisterium adopted this account. As *Ordinatio sacerdotalis* would say, it is "because Christ established things in this way" that "the Church has no authority whatsoever to confer priestly ordination on women." The thesis of the other account is that the Church's practice represents an unexamined way of acting dictated by historical and cultural prejudices against women and sustained by appeal to certain Pauline texts. *Inter insigniores* rejects this account.

The declaration sets out to show that the tradition was not unexamined, and that those who came to its defense appealed not only to Saint Paul but also to the Lord's will for the priesthood, known by way of his choice of the Twelve. In order to counter the view that the Lord himself was constrained to choose men as his apostles by societal and religious expectations, it points to his remarkable freedom, in associating with women, to break with the customs of his day. In addition, it points out that the apostles, who had women collaborators in the service of the Gospel and who were not constrained by the same cultural expectations in a Greek milieu, faithfully observed the Lord's will in this matter. The real reason that the Church reserves priestly ordination to men, it concludes, is her desire to remain faithful to the type of ministry willed by Christ and maintained by the apostles. This tradition constitutes a permanent norm for the admission of candidates to the ministerial priesthood.

Ordinatio sacerdotalis supplements this defense of the tradition by insisting again on Christ's "sovereign freedom" and by calling attention to evidence that he deliberately chose only men when he called the apostles "in accordance with God's plan." It underlines the specific and intimate association of the apostles with the Lord's mission, their vocation to "represent" him, and their fidelity to his will in choosing "fellow workers who would succeed them in their ministry." Both documents recall the classic defense: because even the Blessed Virgin did not receive this vocation, it is clear that the choice of men alone does not imply a negative judgment on women.

THE CHURCH'S CONSTANT TRADITION CAN BE TRACED

The tradition of reserving priestly ordination to men is unbroken and unanimous in the Catholic Church. If ever women were allowed to exercise priestly functions, this innovation was quickly denounced; those who persisted in it were cut off from communion and their views rejected as heretical. This tradition has been so solid that it has never required an explicit formulation by the magisterium. In the Middle Ages, Scholastic theologians proposed arguments to explain and defend it, but they took the practice of the Church for granted, relying on the canonical tradition as normative and as a theological source.[1]

---

1. See John Hilary Martin, "The Injustice of Not Ordaining Women: A Problem for Medieval Theologians," *Theological Studies* 48:2 (June 1987): 303–316, at 303.

The sources cited as evidence in *Inter insigniores* (art. 1) were familiar to students of Catholic theology when the topic was raised in the 1960s. Van der Meer had put these sources in question in 1962. He acknowledged that the tradition was constant and unanimous, but suggested that the Fathers and Doctors of the Church who contributed to its defense all assumed that women are inferior to men and "subject" to them. It is not surprising, then, that the defenders found support for their judgment in the New Testament (see 1 Corinthians 14:33–34; 1 Timothy 2:12). If a faulty view of women dominated their thinking, he argued, it is likely that the reservation of Holy Orders to men is no more than a human tradition.

In recognition of this critique, the declaration concedes that some of the patristic witnesses were influenced by "prejudices unfavorable to women," and that some of the theological arguments proposed by the medieval Doctors "to clarify by reason the data of faith" must be rejected today for the same reason.[2] According to the *Commentary*[3] that accompanied the declaration, the Church has abandoned explanations that "find their basis in an inferiority of women vis-à-vis men" or reveal that their authors "deduced from the teaching of Scripture that woman was 'in a state of submission,' and was incapable of exercising functions of government."[4] *Inter insigniores* maintains that the Church no longer resorts to such explanations, but relies on the tradition of practice itself, and on another line of argument, one that explicitly denies the exercise of priestly functions to women on the basis of Christ's will and example.

The Reactions to Gnostic and Montanist Innovations

We learn from Irenaeus (+ca. 202) and Tertullian (+ca. 225) that some Christian Gnostics and Marcionites of the second century admitted women to priestly functions. Irenaeus condemns, without appealing to scripture, the behavior of Marcus, a sorcerer who invited a woman

---

2. *Inter insigniores*, 1.

3. The official *Commentary*, released along with *Inter insigniores*, does not have the same authority as the declaration, but helps explain its reasoning.

4. *Commentary*, 59, 70.

to consecrate the cup offered to "Charis" (Grace) in a Gnostic religious service. Tertullian denounces certain women among the Gnostics who have the impudence "to teach, to dispute, to enact exorcisms, to offer cures—perhaps even to baptize." He accuses them of disregarding Paul's injunctions (see 1 Corinthians 14:34–35; 1 Timothy 2:12).[5]

Firmilian of Caesarea (+256), Origen (+ca. 250), and Epiphanius of Salamis (+403) all register objections to the activity of women heretics among the Montanists. Firmilian is concerned about the probable invalidity of Baptisms performed by a woman heretic, and Origen about women prophets among the Montanists. In his commentary on 1 Corinthians 14:34–35, Origen maintains that Paul intended to rule out all public teaching by women in church. Neither says anything about ordination.

The first undisputed witness of patristic opposition to the priestly ordination of women is the fourth-century bishop, Saint Epiphanius of Salamis. His testimony is found in a catalogue of heresies called the "Medicine Chest" (Panarion). He too has heard that women function as bishops and presbyters among the Montanists, and he condemns this on the basis of the Pauline ban. According to Epiphanius, the Montanists cite the scriptures not only in support of the prophetic ministry of women (in the line of Eve, Moses' sister Miriam, and the four unmarried daughters of Philip mentioned in Acts 8:21), but also in support of the priestly ordination of women. Montanists, according to Epiphanius, appeal to Galatians 3:28 and to the example of Eve, who was the first to eat from the tree of wisdom, when they should instead attend to Genesis 3:16 and to the instruction of the apostle, that is, to Paul's doctrine regarding the "order of creation" (1 Timothy 2:12; 1 Corinthians 11:8; 1 Timothy 2:14) and his ban on women's teaching and exercising authority over men.

Both Gnostics and Montanists justify their practice by citing Galatians 3:28 and both understand it to mean that the difference between the sexes has been abolished in Christ. Some second-century Gnostic "Gospels" depict Peter and the other apostles debating with Mary Magdalene and Jesus' other women disciples over leadership in

---

5. Tertullian also wrote (De virginibus velandis 9:7): "It is forbidden for a woman to speak in church; she is also not allowed to teach, to baptize, to sacrifice or to presume to the rank of male office, not to mention priestly service." Cited from Hauke, 407.

the Christian community after the Resurrection.[6] According to these sources, Jesus supported the women's right to preach and baptize. The blurring of male-female distinctions in the "androgynous utopia" of the Gnostics led also to the blurring of clergy-lay distinctions, and thus to the admission of women to official functions. The Montanists allowed women with spiritual gifts to participate in public teaching and in the liturgy; they found biblical precedents in the Old and New Testament prophetesses. In addition to claiming that sexual difference was overcome in Christ, the Montanists favored the charismatic leadership of Christian prophets and saints over the governance of bishops ordained in apostolic succession. Their prophets supplemented the apostolic tradition with new revelations and challenged both the authority of the bishops and the doctrine of apostolic succession.

The Theological Analysis of Saint Epiphanius

The response of Saint Epiphanius to Montanism does not exhaust his teaching on the subject. In another context, his defense of the Church's tradition includes an appeal to the divine plan of salvation and to Jesus' deliberate choice of men, and not women, for the apostolic ministry. This is arguably the most important piece of patristic testimony. Epiphanius develops this second line of reasoning, also based on scripture, in conjunction with his denunciation of the female priesthood of the Collyridians. In this sect, women offered small loaves *(kollurida)* in sacrifice to the name of Mary the Ever-Virgin. Epiphanius sets out to condemn their practice of worshipping Mary, but he takes the occasion to explain that women have never been called to offer sacrifice, that is, to be priests.

In the space of several pages, he points out that no women served as priests in the Old Covenant, and that in the New Covenant, its fulfillment, there are again no women priests. Then he states his case: "If women had been directed by God to offer sacrifice *(hierateuein)* or to perform some ecclesiastical office, it would have been more proper to Mary than to anyone else in the New Testament to exercise

---

6. See Elisabeth Schüssler Fiorenza, "Word, Spirit, and Power," in *Women of Spirit*, ed. Eleanor McLaughlin and Rosemary Ruether (Boston: Beacon Press, 1979): 29–70.

a priestly role."[7] Despite the fact that she bore the Son of God in her womb, however, God did not choose priesthood for Mary, nor did he entrust Baptism to her. If he had, Christ would have gone to her rather than John to be baptized. Epiphanius identifies the apostles (the Twelve, plus Paul and Barnabas) and those entrusted with the mysteries (including James, the first bishop of Jerusalem). He then explains that *the Lord called no woman to be one of the Twelve, nor was a woman ever appointed to succeed the apostles as bishop or presbyter.* Christ did not entrust the dignity of the priesthood to his mother; neither did he invite any of the other holy women named in the Gospel—Salome, Martha and Mary, Mary Magdalene, Joanna, Susanna, the Canaanite woman, the woman with the hemorrhage, or any others—to fulfill this role.[8]

Epiphanius bears witness, then, to the tradition that God's will regarding the female priesthood is known by means of Christ's choice of the Twelve. He acknowledges that women may engage in prophecy and serve in the ecclesiastical office of deaconess, but insists that they have never been admitted to the priesthood. The reason is not their "subject" status or some unworthiness deriving from their sex; it is a dispensation of the Lord's will.

Epiphanius is also the first to point to the unbroken tradition itself as an argument,[9] but he is not the first to link the vocation to priesthood with the call of the Twelve, nor to imply that bishops and presbyters are the successors to the apostles. These connections were already well established in the patristic tradition. In fact, the argument that juxtaposes Christ's choice of the Twelve with his failure to choose Mary and the other holy women is not original with him, but dates back to the mid-third century and earlier, and is found in the type of materials cited next by *Inter insigniores.*

---

7. The translations of patristic texts are from J. Kevin Coyle, "The Fathers on Women and Women's Ordination," *Église et théologie* 9:1 (January 1978), 82–83.

8. *Panarion* 79, 7, 3–4.

9. According to Hauke (p. 418), Epiphanius describes female priesthood not only as a breach of Church discipline but also as heresy.

The Ancient Canonical Tradition

There are ancient "Church orders" and collections of ecclesiastical canons that supply further evidence. Together, the *Didascalia Apostolorum (The Instruction of the Apostles)*, a Syriac document of the mid-third century, and the *Constitutiones Apostolicae (Apostolic Constitutions)*, a late-fourth-century document that includes a reworking of much of the *Didascalia*, testify to the ban on teaching and baptizing by women and the prohibition of their ordination to the priesthood. These two references are of special interest because they appeal to the "command" of Christ and the "law of the Gospel." Like the *Panarion* of Epiphanius, the *Didascalia* and the *Apostolic Constitutions* justify the tradition of reserving priestly ordination to men on the grounds that it is the will of Christ.

Both of these texts belong to the genre of pseudo-apostolic literature, that is, they are compilations attributed to the apostles, and the authors speak in the name of the Twelve. They report that Jesus did not appoint either his mother or his women disciples to share in certain tasks; women who assume these tasks, then, violate the "commandment of the Lord"[10] and act against the "law of the Gospel." For example, in the *Didascalia* we read that women are not to teach in the Church; if Jesus had wanted his women disciples to teach, he would have commanded them to go out with the Twelve. It is also a "violation of the commandment" for women to baptize; if it were lawful, Jesus would have sought Baptism from his mother rather than from John. According to the *Apostolic Constitutions*, Mary and the women of Jesus' company are not permitted to teach because the Lord sent not them but the Twelve. If teaching and baptizing are prohibited, it asks, how much more is "exercising a priestly office *(hierateusai)* inconsistent with [woman's] nature?" And if the Lord did not command this, it is "because he knew the arrangement of nature . . . being as he was the architect of nature and the legislator of the commandment."[11]

Within this argument are embedded some important assumptions. First, the ministry of bishops and priests is clearly

---

10. Hauke (pp. 363–396) proposes that this may refer to the "command" mentioned in 1 Corinthians 14:37.

11. *The Apostolic Constitutions* III.9 (Coyle, p. 92). In this era, baptizing and preaching were reserved to the bishop.

understood to carry forward the apostolic charge given to the Twelve; exclusion from the Twelve implies exclusion from these offices. Second, Mary's dignity and the women disciples' holiness are presumed to recommend them as candidates for ordination; the fact that they were not chosen, then, is not dictated by a deficiency on their part, even though it is related to their "nature." Because the Lord did not call even his mother to belong to the Twelve, despite her great dignity and excellence, it is inferred that he did not intend women to assume priestly functions. Third, the inclusive character of Jesus' company is confirmed: it was not for lack of eligible candidates that the Lord did not entrust sacerdotal functions to women. And fourth, the Lord, as the author of human nature and the giver of the law, knows best how to assign responsibilities in his community.

It is not just an occasional argument that favors this second explanation. As the declaration points out, the patristic sources appeal not only to the Pauline texts but also to the will of Christ, the unbroken tradition of sacramental practice, and the doctrine of apostolic succession according to which priestly ordination gives some participation in the role of the Twelve.

The Testimony of Medieval Theologians

The medieval witnesses, including the Scholastic doctors, are unanimous in their opinion that women cannot be admitted to priestly ordination. Some canonists and theologians explicitly affirm that the attempted ordination of a woman would be not only illicit but also invalid. Certain of them cite as evidence Jesus' choice of 12 males as his apostles and employ the ancient argument of the Blessed Virgin's exclusion from the Twelve to show that his decision did not suggest any lack of personal dignity or holiness on the part of women. This latter argument continued to be influential because it had found a place in the canonical collection of Decretals. Here, it was handed on in the formulation given it by Pope Innocent III in 1210: "Although the Blessed Virgin Mary was of higher dignity and excellence than all the Apostles, it was to them, not her, that the Lord entrusted the keys of the kingdom of heaven."[12] From Duns Scotus (+1308) forward, other

---

12. *Commentary*, 60. This became a *locus communis* for canonical commentaries.

Scholastic theologians taught that the prohibition of women's ordination to the priesthood was based neither on the subject status of women nor on the symbolism of the sexes but on a historic determination by Christ.[13]

Another line of reasoning, familiar to students of theology from its presence in the argumentation of Saint Thomas Aquinas (+1274), depends more directly on the teaching of Saint Paul and finds there not only an explicit ban on women's participation in certain ministerial roles but also a biblical theology of the respective places of men and women in the orders of creation and salvation. The declaration notes the presence here of theological arguments "that modern thought would have difficulty in admitting or would even rightly reject." Without dismissing the witness of Saint Paul or Saint Thomas, it focuses instead on the ancient witness that appeals to the deliberate character of the Lord's choice of 12 men.[14]

The Tradition Is Rooted in Jesus' Way of Acting

Inter insigniores proceeds to consider the evidence found in the Gospels.[15] Because we have no "saying" of the Lord that explicitly interprets his intention, we must consider instead the implications of his "way of acting," namely, the evidence that "Jesus Christ did not call any woman to become part of the Twelve."

In the early stages of the debate on the ordination of women, scholars commonly regarded this appeal to Jesus' choice of men as a rather weak argument. Those who proposed it as a reason were chided as naive for their failure to acknowledge that the Lord could not have done differently. Given the status of women in first-century Judaism, this reasoning went, it would have been virtually impossible

---

13. See John Hilary Martin, "The Ordination of Women and the Theologians in the Middle Ages," in *A History of Women and Ordination*, vol. 1: *The Ordination of Women in a Medieval Context*, ed. Bernard Cooke and Gary Macy (Lanham, Maryland: Scarecrow Press, 2002): 31–175.

14. According to Louis Ligier, "Women and the Ministerial Priesthood," *Origins* 7:14 (April 20, 1978): 694–702, at 696, the Congregation for the Doctrine of the Faith deliberately bracketed the Pauline prescriptions.

15. Article 2.

for him to call the women of his company to the apostolic ministry. Because the testimony of women was not accepted in the law, for example, they could not have served the essential apostolic function of bearing witness to the Resurrection.[16] With the change in women's status, it was argued, this obstacle has been eliminated.

His Sovereign Freedom

Further reflection on the implications of the Gospel evidence, however, sheds fresh light on the evangelical newness of Jesus' teaching and example with respect to women. Today, scholars who compare the Gospel record of Jesus' way of acting with the religious and cultural norms of first-century Judaism emphasize that Jesus did *not* conform to these expectations. On the contrary, he directly broke with the religious and cultural norms of his time when he mingled freely and publicly with women, included them in his company, conversed with them openly about the things of God, disregarded the laws of ritual purity, accepted their ministrations, and so on. If Jesus did not share the prejudices of his contemporaries, it would appear that he "could have" entrusted the apostolic charge to women if he had wished to, but freely chose to do otherwise.

The declaration, making precisely this claim, recounts Gospel examples that illustrate Jesus' surprising freedom with respect to the customs of his day. Pope John Paul II subsequently identified this as the "Gospel innovation" that grounds contemporary Catholic teaching on the equality of women and men. He firmly reasserts the same point in *Ordinatio sacerdotalis:* the Lord was not constrained by the historical and cultural expectations of his time in his relations vis-à-vis women. When he chose only men as his apostles, therefore, he acted with "sovereign freedom" and with deliberate intent.

The magisterium also cites with approval the patristic reasoning that Jesus' failure to choose even his mother to belong to the Twelve represents his will with respect to women in general. This is taken as proof that his choice was not governed by a low estimation of women. The magisterium favors the "Mariological" version of this argument perhaps because this is the form in which it has survived both

---

16. See Van der Meer, 14.

in the Eastern Churches and in the canonical tradition of the Latin West that influenced Scholastic theological reflection. The versions that point out that Jesus did not lack women disciples, and could have sent *them* if he wanted to, should also be kept in mind, because they respond more directly to the questions raised by contemporary biblical exegetes about Jesus' intention.

The Symbolism of the Twelve

The declaration and *Ordinatio sacerdotalis* are cautious when they imply that Jesus "could have" entrusted the "apostolic charge" to women. The declaration acknowledges the questions raised by biblical scholars regarding the symbolism of the Twelve and their relation to "the apostles." It anticipates a common objection when it asserts, in a footnote, that the symbolism of the Twelve is not limited to representing the 12 patriarchs of Israel, and that their vocation is not limited to judging the 12 tribes of Israel at the end of time (see Matthew 19:28; Luke 22:30).[17] It concludes that "the essential meaning of the choice of the Twelve should be sought in the totality of their mission (see Mark 3:14): they are to represent Jesus to the people and carry on his work."

    Ordinatio sacerdotalis supplies additional evidence for this claim by focusing attention on the deliberation that preceded the call of the apostles and on their office as Jesus' representatives.[18] In the accounts of their vocation, Jesus is depicted as spending the night in prayer to the Father (Luke 6:12). He is said to have chosen "those whom he wanted" (Mark 3:13–14), and his choice is attributed to the work of the Holy Spirit (Acts 1:2). In faith, the Church sees here the fulfillment of a divine plan, not a concession to cultural constraints. The 12 men are called by Jesus "to be with him," to share his mission, and to carry on his saving work by his authority. They are the foundation of the Church (see Ephesians 2:20; Revelation 21:14). The magisterium clearly assumes that "the call to belong to the Twelve" has implications for "the call to the ordained ministry." The Church believes that priestly ordination hands on to others the office entrusted

---

17. *Inter insigniores*, note 10, and the *Commentary*, 63–64.
18. See Vanhoye, 151–157.

by Christ to his apostles, that is, a share in their "apostolic ministry" of teaching, sanctifying, and governing the faithful.

"Convergent Indications" Support This Tradition

As the declaration observes, the evidence from the Gospel tradition does not make it "immediately obvious" that the Lord intended to entrust the "apostolic charge" only to men, but it provides "a number of convergent indications" that support this conclusion.[19] In any event, "a purely historical exegesis of the texts cannot suffice" to establish Christ's will on this matter. The Church must also consult the tradition, and the tradition sees in his example with respect to the Twelve an expression of his will for the ordained ministry. The *Commentary* reinforces the point: the New Testament, on its own, cannot answer the question about women's possible accession to the ministerial priesthood, just as it cannot, on its own, provide an adequate account of the institution of the rest of the sacraments.[20] The determination of Christ's will regarding these things comes about through a process in which the Church consults both scripture and tradition.[21]

THE APOSTLES' WAY OF ACTING CONFIRMS THE TRADITION

The declaration asserts that the apostolic community "remained faithful to the attitude of Jesus towards women."[22] At the same time, its leaders continued to observe the Lord's will with respect to the Twelve and the apostolic ministry. The declaration provides three illustrations. First, when it came time to replace Judas, only men *(andres)* were deemed eligible (Acts 1:21), despite the fact that the Virgin Mary occupied a privileged place in the community. Second, on Pentecost the public proclamation of the Gospel was made only by

---

19. See Guy Mansini, "On Affirming a Dominical Intention of a Male Priesthood," *The Thomist* 61:2 (April 1997): 301–316. Mansini argues that the Lord's implicit intention, which later came to light under questioning, can be discerned by assembling theological elements and analyses known to all theologians.

20. CCC § 1117.

21. *Commentary*, 62.

22. *Inter insigniores*, 3.

Peter and the Eleven (Acts 2:14), despite the fact that the Holy Spirit had descended on a large gathering of men and women (Acts 2:1; 1:14). Third, although the spread of the Gospel to the Gentile world entailed the abandonment of many Mosaic practices, and although the status of women in the Hellenistic world would have allowed for their admission to public ministry, and although many women were engaged with Paul in the service of the Gospel, there is no evidence that women received a commission to the apostolic ministry by a "laying on of hands."[23] In other words, in the Hellenistic milieu the apostles could have done otherwise, if fidelity to the Lord's will had not held them back. *Ordinatio sacerdotalis* does not repeat these arguments, except to note that when the apostles chose "fellow workers who would succeed them in their ministry," they acknowledged the Lord's "way of acting" as a norm by choosing only men. In a footnote, it cites 1 Timothy 3:1–13, 2 Timothy 1:6, and Titus 1:5–9.

THE TRADITION HAS NORMATIVE VALUE

As we have seen, the belief that the Lord intended to entrust the apostolic ministry to men and not to women was preserved by means of a tradition of practice. The belief itself was articulated in response to innovations that were judged to depart from Christ's will and from the plan of God. Theologians searched the biblical evidence and proposed explanations for the tradition. Bishops, as guardians of the Church's apostolic faith and order, ruled on the question to safeguard that faith and to maintain discipline, and their judgments found their way into a growing body of canonical legislation. This entire process took place within a community whose members believed that the Lord Jesus had appointed apostles to carry on his ministry of teaching, sanctifying, and shepherding the rest of the baptized, and that the apostles in turn had entrusted this charge to their coworkers and successors by a laying on of hands and invocation of the Holy Spirit, a rite that was eventually counted as one of the seven sacraments.

The magisterium has reaffirmed that the tradition of reserving priestly ordination to men constitutes a permanent norm. It is not

---

23. The declaration speaks of "conferring ordination," but Vanhoye (p. 154) uses the expression "laying on of hands."

simply a question of ecclesiastical discipline; it is a doctrinal tradition that pertains to the deposit of the faith. The Church's "practice" is, in this case, a *sacramental* practice. If the Catholic Church attaches doctrinal importance to the question of women's ordination it is because she teaches that Holy Orders is a sacrament, and that the ministerial (or "hierarchical") priesthood conferred by this sacrament belongs to the essential constitution of the Church.

This Doctrine Pertains to the Nature of Holy Orders as a Sacrament

In explaining why the reservation of priestly ordination to men is a permanent norm, the declaration factors in the Catholic doctrine that Holy Orders is a sacrament. The belief that the substance of the sacramental signs is given by Christ constitutes an important element in the judgment that this tradition cannot be changed by the Church.[24] In order to understand *Ordinatio sacerdotalis* and the formulation of doctrine regarding the recipient of Holy Orders in the *Catechism of the Catholic Church* (§ 1577), it is necessary to appreciate the implications of this claim. As we have pointed out, the rejection of Holy Orders as a sacrament by the sixteenth-century Reformers affects how Protestants evaluate the question.

According to Catholic doctrine, the sacraments are "efficacious signs of grace, instituted by Christ and entrusted to the Church, by which divine life is dispensed to us."[25] If Holy Orders fulfills this definition, then ordination is considerably more than a public rite of installation into an ecclesiastical "leadership role," and more than a rite instituted by the Church, in which its officers give certain worthy and capable baptized persons a public commission to do for other believers what any of the baptized could in principle do.[26] Catholic doctrine entails a particular understanding of the sign, its efficacy, and its institution by the Lord—its "dominical institution."

---

24. This is the reason that the Church's power over them is limited. See the Council of Trent, Session XXI, chapter two (DS 1728; ND 1324), and Pope Pius XII's apostolic constitution *Sacramentum ordinis* (DS 3857).

25. CCC § 1131.

26. See Congregation for the Doctrine of the Faith, "The Minister of the Eucharist," *Origins* 13 (September 15, 1983): 229–233 (ND 1756–1757).

In the first place, the substance of the sacramental signs given by Christ is linked to "the deep symbolism of actions and things." As the declaration recalls, the "signs" are natural, but their symbolism is rooted in the history of salvation. The sacraments refer us "to constitutive events of Christianity and to Christ himself."[27] When challenges to the Church's practice arose, its defenders appealed not only to "natural" differences between men and women that might be held to dictate their appropriate social roles, but also to the Gospel accounts of the Lord's choice of the Twelve and its confirmation by the practice of the apostles.

If the Lord chose men and not women to belong to the Twelve, we must assume that he had some reason. This is not arbitrary but significant. In sacramental theology, the determination of the "subject" or recipient of the sacrament belongs to its institution by Christ and to its constitution as a sign. In the language of sacramental theology, the "matter" of the ordination rite is the laying on of hands, and the "form" is the prayer of consecration. The recipient, or "subject," of the sacrament, however, is also a constitutive part of the outward sign. For example, the "subjects" of the sacrament of Marriage are a baptized man and a baptized woman. The "subject" of the Anointing of the Sick is a baptized person in need of healing or strengthening in view of illness, advanced age, or imminent death due to sickness. The "subject" of priestly ordination is a baptized male. When the declaration explains that the Church is not authorized to ordain women because she is not free to change the "sign" designated by the Lord, it refers to the "subject" of the sacrament.[28] We know that this tradition is important because the Church's pastors claim to be bound by it and teach that the attempted ordination of women is not only illicit but also invalid.

Second, the sacraments are distinguished from other ecclesiastical rites like "sacramentals" insofar as they were instituted by Christ. As theologians came to understand and classify Holy Orders as a sacrament, they traced its "dominical institution" back to Christ's call

---

27. *Inter insigniores*, 4.

28. Just as the Church cannot substitute some other food and drink for bread and wine in the Eucharist, because the Lord himself designated these elements, so she has no authority to change this sign. See the *Commentary*, 68.

of the "Twelve Apostles." The Council of Trent identified the institution of the priesthood with the command to "Do this" given them by the Lord at the Last Supper.[29] Today, theologians—without excluding this teaching—also look beyond that single occasion and beyond that single facet of the apostolic ministry, for they are concerned to illuminate the Council's teaching concerning its sacramental nature. They look as well to a series of events, ranging from the original call of the Twelve to the missionary mandate and the descent of the Holy Spirit at Pentecost. In other words, they point out how Christ's institution of the sacrament is located within and linked to his institution of the apostolic (that is, hierarchical) ministry.[30]

Third, the sacraments are "efficacious signs" that bestow divine grace on those who receive them. Catholics believe that Holy Orders "configures the recipient to Christ by a special grace of the Holy Spirit, so that he may serve as Christ's instrument for the Church."[31] Ordination confers on bishops and priests not only "a function which could . . . be exercised by any member of the Church,"[32] but the "sacred power" to carry out the Lord's own ministry of teaching, sanctifying, and governing by his authority and in his "person." This configuration to Christ is distinct from the one already received in Baptism; it is a different gift of grace ordered to the service of the rest of the baptized.[33]

According to Catholic doctrine, a Christian who has not received this sacrament is incapable of celebrating sacraments that require the "character" of Holy Orders, for example, the Eucharist and the sacrament of Penance. To act with the authority of Christ in his capacity as the Head of the Church, one must be "authorized" and equipped by Christ. This takes place by means of the sacrament of Holy Orders, a gift by which the Lord makes his own ministry available to his people through the ministry of bishops and priests.

---

29. Council of Trent, Session XXII (DS 1740, 1752; ND 1546, 1556) and Session XXIII (DS 1764, 1771; ND 1707, 1713).

30. See the International Theological Commission, "The Priestly Ministry" and "Catholic Teaching on Apostolic Succession," in *Texts and Documents 1969–1985* (San Francisco: Ignatius Press, 1989), 3–87, at 36–41, and 93–104, at 97–103.

31. CCC § 1581.

32. *Ordinatio sacerdotalis,* 2.

33. See CCC § 1547.

This Concerns the Constitution of the Church

According to *Ordinatio sacerdotalis* (art. 4), the question of women's ordination "pertains to the Church's divine constitution itself." What we have just said about the Catholic understanding of Holy Orders as a sacrament may help point out the connection. The Second Vatican Council taught that "the bishops have by divine institution taken the place of the Apostles as pastors of the Church."[34] The divine institution that provides for bishops in apostolic succession is the same institution, viewed from another angle, as that which brought the sacrament of Holy Orders into being.

In *Lumen gentium*, chapter three, the Fathers of the Second Vatican Council teach that the bishops are successors of the apostles "by divine institution," and that this office is conferred on them by means of a sacrament, not by a juridical appointment from the Pope. According to the Council, episcopal ordination incorporates a bishop into the episcopal college of which the bishop of Rome, the Pope, is the head.

The Fathers of Vatican II were concerned to complete the teaching of the First Vatican Council (1869–1870) about the vocation and office of Peter.[35] Its one-sided focus on papal primacy and infallibility had brought about a need to clarify the role of bishops and the episcopal college vis-à-vis the papacy. The Second Vatican Council's teaching on the hierarchical constitution of the Church, therefore, places new emphasis on the other apostles, apostolic succession, and the apostolic college in order to flesh out the post–Vatican I ecclesiology dominated by Peter.

The Council's teaching has a bearing on our question, first, insofar as it makes formal and repeated assertions about the Lord's intention with regard to handing on the apostolic ministry, which it identifies as making his own ministry present and available in the Church down through the ages. Setting out its doctrine of episcopacy in *Lumen gentium*, the Council teaches that the apostles[36] received

---

34. *Lumen gentium*, 20.

35. The Franco-Prussian War interrupted this Council's work on the constitution of the Church and it was never completed.

36. The Council documents do not discriminate, as critical scholarship does, between the Twelve and the apostles.

a mandate from Christ himself, which they then handed on to their collaborators and successors by a laying on of hands. The Council had no hesitation in speaking of Christ's intention to provide this apostolic ministry for the Church.[37]

The teaching of *Lumen gentium* also has a bearing on the reservation of priestly ordination to men when it focuses attention on the episcopal college. The Church is not built on Peter alone, but also on the apostles who shepherd the flock together with him. The Lord Jesus formed the Twelve into a "college," or permanent assembly. The Council draws an analogy between the college of bishops with the Pope as its head and the apostolic college with Peter as its head.[38] The point is to show that all of the bishops have a role to play in the governance of the universal Church "with and under Peter." This doctrine, too, calls attention to the significance of the Twelve.[39]

The implications for our question of the Council's contributions to ecclesiology become clear in the *Catechism's* explanation of why women cannot be ordained (§ 1577):

> "Only a baptized man *(vir)* validly receives sacred ordination."[40] The Lord Jesus chose men *(viri)* to form the college of the twelve apostles, and the apostles did the same when they chose collaborators to succeed them in their ministry. *The college of bishops*, with whom the priests are united in the priesthood, *makes the college of the twelve an ever-present and ever-active reality until Christ's return.* The Church recognizes herself to be bound by this choice made by the Lord himself. For this reason the ordination of women is not possible.[41]

We find the teaching of *Inter insigniores* here, but the reason for not admitting women is extended, as it were, by the reference to the ongoing role of the Twelve—carried out by their successors— in the life of the Church.[42] This rather sober, ecclesiological formulation directs attention to the vocation and symbolism of

---

37. For a recent evaluation, see Sullivan, *From Apostles to Bishops*.

38. *Lumen gentium*, preliminary explanatory note 1.

39. The scholarly research that paved the way for this doctrinal affirmation paid close attention to the biblical and patristic evidence for a collegial exercise of the apostolic ministry.

40. *Codex iuris canonici*, canon 1024.

41. Emphasis added.

42. See *Lumen gentium*, 20. See also CCC § 860.

the Twelve, and to its importance for the constitution of the Church. It is by way of Jesus' choice of 12 men that we know his will for the apostolic ministry of bishops and priests. No other appeal is made. It assumes that the college of bishops carries forward the vocation given to the college of the Twelve. It does not say that bishops and priests are chosen from among men in order to represent Jesus who is male— only that they must be men to represent in the midst of the Church the Twelve whom he chose and sent out to carry on his ministry.

CONCLUSION

The Church's living tradition provides the proper context for discovering Christ's will. One could imagine that things might be arranged differently,[43] but ecclesial discernment is rooted in the concrete events of biblical revelation and is bound by fidelity to Christ's manner of acting. The declaration cites the case of the Eucharist. The Eucharist is not only a community meal; it is also a memorial that "makes present and actual Christ's sacrifice and his offering by the Church."[44] Similarly, the priestly ministry is "not just a pastoral service; it ensures the continuity of the functions entrusted by Christ to the Apostles and the continuity of the powers related to those functions."

In the declaration and *Ordinatio sacerdotalis*, the belief that Holy Orders is a sacrament and that the bishops are the successors of the apostles functions as a premise; this belongs to the Church's "settled doctrine" regarding the ministerial priesthood and the constitution of the Church. For Catholics, the question of women's ordination cannot be treated in isolation from these other doctrines. We should be wary of any proposal that calls them into question. In fact, the issue of ordaining women to the priesthood is integrally linked to them. It "pertains" to them in such a way that questions raised about this also touch on them.

---

43. See the *Commentary*, 68.
44. *Inter insigniores*, 4.

Chapter 5

The Church's Theological Arguments

In chapter four, we took a closer look at the fundamental reasons the Church gives for regarding the tradition of reserving priestly ordination to men. The magisterium claims that Jesus' choice of men as his apostles is the "essential reason" for the tradition. It notes that his remarkable freedom from convention in relating to women, as witnessed in the Gospels, supports the belief that in choosing only men for this role he acted freely and deliberately. And it appeals to the example of the apostles, who followed the Lord's example in handing on the apostolic charge only to men. The Pauline texts that have traditionally been invoked as evidence that women are in a state of subjection, and therefore should not exercise authority over men, are not introduced into this account of the fundamental reasons. The magisterium asserts that the Church's unbroken tradition of practice has a normative character because it is based on Christ's example and has always been considered "to conform to God's plan for his Church."[1]

ARGUMENTS BASED ON THE "ANALOGY OF FAITH"

Once it is agreed that the Lord's example establishes a permanent norm for the priesthood, the inquiry as to why he chose only men takes on a positive character. The theological arguments attempt to clarify the doctrine by the "analogy of faith,"[2] that is, to discover its "fittingness"

---

1. *Inter insigniores*, 4.
2. CCC § 114 defines this as "the coherence of the truths of faith among themselves and within the whole plan of Revelation."

or appropriateness by examining it in relationship to other doctrines. In order to engage in a method of theological reasoning that illuminates one doctrine by means of others, it is necessary to be familiar with these other doctrines, the theological tradition that interprets them, and the authority with which they are taught. The certainty the Church has about some doctrines justifies using them as a guide for the investigation of more obscure questions. In accord with this method, then, the magisterium relies on certain settled doctrines of the Church and the common teaching of Catholic theologians as points of reference.

The two "theological arguments" proposed by the declaration take their bearings from the doctrine of the ministerial priesthood. The first explores its relation to the mystery of Christ, and the second, to the mystery of the Church. We have anticipated the second argument—the ecclesiological argument—in chapter three,[3] so we will limit our considerations here to the Christological argument. This was first proposed in *Inter insigniores* (art. 5). About ten years later, Pope John Paul II clarified it further, in response to the feminist critique, in *Mulieris dignitatem*. Then in 1992 he introduced the same argument into a synthetic restatement of the doctrine of the ministerial priesthood in *Pastores dabo vobis*.

THE CHRISTOLOGICAL ARGUMENT IN *INTER INSIGNIORES*

According to the declaration, it is fitting that men and not women are called to the ministerial priesthood because the sacrament of Holy Orders has a specific reference to the mystery of Christ who was and remains a man. This argument may seem to be merely an appeal to common sense, in accord with the logic, for instance, of a theatrical production in which ordinarily a director casts a male in a male role. The director relies on the "natural symbolism" of gender. The argument, however, is in fact theological. It is developed in accordance with commonly accepted principles of sacramental theology and it draws on the biblical symbolism of the mystery of the covenant.

---

3. See chapter three.

The declaration explains the fittingness of the Lord's choice in three steps. First, the priest acts "in the person of Christ" *(in persona Christi)* in certain sacramental functions. Second, the formula *in persona Christi* implies that the priest is himself a "sign," as understood in sacramental theology. And third, because he is a sign of Christ, who was and remains a man *(vir)*, it is fitting that the priest be a man.[4] In the context of this third step, the declaration proposes its argument, based on the biblical motif of the covenant, regarding the sacramental significance of the maleness of Christ, and of the priest as his living image. The covenant relationship between God and humanity and between Christ and the Church is expressed eloquently in the scriptures by analogy with marriage, the "covenant" of love between a man and a woman. Because the analogy implies—and indeed depends on— an understanding of the complementarity of the sexes as ordered to marriage, that understanding as elaborated in Christian anthropology will find a place in theological reflection on the reasons for the Lord's choice of men and not women as his apostles.

The Priest Acts *in Persona Christi*

Theological reflection discovers the Church's practice to be profoundly fitting because the priest, in the exercise of his sacramental ministry, represents Christ. When he performs actions that require the character of Holy Orders the priest acts not in his own name, *in persona propria,* but rather in the person of Christ, *in persona Christi.* This is the "Church's constant teaching," declared by Saint Paul,[5] articulated in the third century by Saint Cyprian of Carthage, developed in medieval theology, and recently repeated and clarified at both the Second Vatican Council and the 1971 Synod of Bishops.[6]

Some priestly functions, in particular, the consecration and offering of the true body and blood of the Lord in the sacrifice of the Eucharist and the forgiveness of sins in the sacrament of Penance, can be effectively accomplished only by one who has received the

---

4. *Commentary,* 70–71.

5. *In persona Christi* was Saint Jerome's Latin translation of Paul's expression in 2 Corinthians 2:10. See 2 Corinthians 5:20 and Galatians 4:14 for Paul's awareness of being the ambassador and representative of Christ.

6. See *Inter insigniores,* note 16.

sacramental character imprinted by Holy Orders.[7] The Church teaches that ordination bestows an indelible "character" on the soul of the one who receives it. This character, the abiding or permanent effect of the sacrament, is a "sacred power" that authorizes and equips the priest to function as an instrument, or "minister," of Christ, the principal agent in the celebration of the sacraments.

According to Catholic doctrine, the sacrament of Holy Orders effects a change in men who are ordained priests.[8] It configures them to Christ, objectively and permanently, as persons "fitted" to be his instruments for the performance of those acts that are properly his.[9] The sacramental character conferred at ordination imparts the radical capacity to act *in persona Christi*,[10] or as the Second Vatican Council specified *in persona Christi Capitis Ecclesiae*, in the person of Christ the Head of the Church.[11] The declaration uses the expression "acting *in persona Christi*" in this technical sense, which has to do with the priest's being constituted an instrument of the Lord's activity in the sacraments.[12]

The Priest Is a Sacramental "Sign" of Christ

The priest's representation of Christ finds its "supreme expression" in the celebration of the Eucharist. Here, the priest acts "not only through the effective power conferred on him by Christ, but *in persona Christi*, taking the role of Christ, to the point of being his very image,

---

7. Council of Trent, Session VII, canon 10 (DS 1610; ND 1320) and Session XXIII, canon 1 (DS 1771; ND 1714).

8. The Council of Trent, Session XXIII, chapter 4 (DS 1767; ND 1710), rejects the view of some Reformers that "all Christians are without distinction priests of the New Testament, or that all are equally endowed with the same spiritual power."

9. See the *Commentary* (p. 71) for an elaboration of this.

10. See Guy Mansini, "Episcopal *Munera* and the Character of Episcopal Order," *The Thomist* 66 (2002): 369–394.

11. See my essay, "Priestly Identity: 'Sacrament' of Christ the Head," *Worship:* 70:4 (July 1996): 290–306, and Guy Mansini, "Sacerdotal Character at the Second Vatican Council," *The Thomist* 67 (2003): 539–577. Mansini shows that the Second Vatican Council did not intend to ground the priest's ministry of teaching and ruling in the character.

12. Ordination also bestows the grace to become configured to Christ by a life of virtue, but a priest can refuse this grace and fall into sin. The sacramental character, by contrast, is a permanent and objective deputation to the Christian cult. Saint Thomas elaborated the distinction between acting *in persona Christi* and acting *in persona Ecclesiae*, in fact, to address the question of the validity of sacraments celebrated by an unworthy priest. See *Summa Theologiae* 3, Q. 82, aa. 5, 7–8.

when he pronounces the words of consecration."[13] The priest, therefore, is not only an "instrument" of Christ; he is also a "sign" of Christ. The declaration appeals to the principle invoked by Saint Thomas when treating our question: "Sacramental signs represent what they signify by natural resemblance." With Saint Thomas, it assumes that the priest himself functions as a sign, and that the natural correspondence of gender has a part to play in this signification. As a result of the properly celebrated sacramental rite, the man himself becomes a "sacrament," that is, a sign, "image," or icon of Christ.[14]

The sacramental character, which is the permanent effect *(res et sacramentum)* of the rite and has to do with its "supernatural effectiveness," is invisible. The outwardly visible sign that represents Christ, then, is the person who has been ordained. The theological argument advances by asserting that "the same natural resemblance is required for persons as for things."[15] As we have already pointed out, the "subject" or recipient of priestly ordination belongs to the sacramental sign.

The Scholastic theologians explained the impossibility of admitting women to the priesthood on the basis of sacramental signification, but they did not all relate this explicitly to the representation of Christ as a male. In fact, Saint Thomas did not do so. His interpretation of women's incapacity for ordination involves an appeal both to the Pauline ban and also to a hierarchical understanding of sexual complementarity: a woman cannot signify "eminence" because she is in a "state of subjection."[16] The declaration follows instead Saint Bonaventure, who argued that priestly ordination is reserved to men because only a man can be the sign of Christ, who is male.[17] According to Bonaventure,

---

13. *Inter insigniores*, 5.

14. See *Inter insigniores*, 5. Saint Thomas does not argue that the priest must be a man because Christ is male, but he appears to assume this correlation when he asserts that the bishop represents Christ as the Bridegroom of the Church. See *Summa contra Gentiles* 4, 74; 4, 76, 7; *Summa Theologiae Supplement*, Q. 40, a. 4 ad 3um, and the *Lectura* on 1 Timothy, c. 3, lect. 1, no. 96.

15. Saint Bonaventure supports this explicitly. See Jean Rezette, "La Sacerdoce et la Femme chez Saint Bonaventure," *Antonianum* 51:4 (October-December 1976): 520–527. Saint Thomas argues that a woman is incompetent to receive Holy Orders in the same way that a healthy person is incompetent to receive Extreme Unction. See *Summa Theologiae Supplement*, Q. 32, a. 2.

16. See the *Commentary*, 59.

17. See note 9.

In this sacrament the ordained person is the sign of Christ the Mediator; since the Mediator belongs only to the male sex, he can only be represented by the male sex; therefore, the capacity for receiving Orders belongs only to males who alone can represent him by nature and, having received the character, can effectively bear the sign [of Christ].[18]

When the declaration asserts that "it would be difficult to see in the minister the image of Christ" unless he were a man, it appeals to this natural symbolism of gender correspondence: a man fittingly represents the male Christ. As an "outward sign," a sacrament should be self-evident, not needing further interpretation. When a man takes the role of Christ in the celebration of the Eucharist, the "natural resemblance" of gender functions as an outward sign that he is acting *in persona Christi Capitis Ecclesiae.* As the declaration points out, the priest functions as a sacramental sign *within the context of another sacrament,* namely, in his capacity as the minister of the Eucharist.[19]

The Priest Is a Sign of Christ, Who Is and Remains a Man

Next, the declaration considers Christ's identity as a male. In the first place, of course, the mystery of the Incarnation is that the Word of God took on flesh (see John 1:14), that is, assumed our human nature, in order to save the world in it. Christ is the "firstborn of all humanity, of women as well as men," and his saving work overcomes the opposition between Jew and Greek, slave and free, male and female: all are one in Christ Jesus (see Galatians 3:28). The Incarnation has to do with humanity as a whole, for the Word of God has, by his Incarnation, united himself in some fashion with every human being.[20]

The primary focus of the Incarnation, then, is clearly that the Word became a human being, rather than that he became a male. In order to be truly human, "like us in everything but sin" (see Hebrews 4:15), however, the human nature assumed by the Word had to be characterized by sex. That the Word took on human nature as a male

---

18. See Bonaventure, *In IV Sent.* d. 25, a.2, q.1, conclusion. Any appeal to Bonaventure must be a "critical retrieval," because his line of argument is not free of ideas prejudicial to women. Bonaventure also notes the objection that a woman cannot be advanced to the episcopate because she is not "the bridegroom of the Church."

19. See *Summa Theologiae* 3, q. 82, a. 1.

20. See *Gaudium et spes,* 22.

is a fact of history. According to the declaration, it has significance not only for his human identity, but also for the economy of salvation.

The declaration discovers the "harmony" or fittingness of the Incarnation according to the male sex by considering God's covenant with the Chosen People as a "nuptial mystery." In the Old Testament, from the time of the prophets forward, God's compassionate love for Israel is depicted as the love of a bridegroom for his beloved bride; it calls for the response of "bridal" love from the covenant partner. God, in fact, is depicted as the Bridegroom of Israel. The declaration appeals to the prophets and to the Jewish and Christian reading of the Song of Songs as evidence of this motif; it also cites biblical texts that show that failure to keep the covenant was interpreted as marital infidelity.[21]

This "nuptial mystery" reached its culmination when Jesus Christ, the Word made flesh, established the New Covenant in his blood. He is the Bridegroom and the Church is the Bride for whom he has sacrificed his life. The declaration discerns this theme in the Pauline corpus (see 2 Corinthians 11:2; Ephesians 5:22–23), John 3:29, and Revelation 19:7, 9. According to the letter to the Ephesians, Christ loves the Church and makes her holy and spotless: "henceforth he is inseparable from her." The theme is also present in the synoptic Gospels. Jesus identifies himself as the Bridegroom in Mark 2:19, Matthew 22:1–14, and parallels.

According to the declaration, the symbolic language of sexuality in the economy of revelation is a bearer of meaning that cannot be disregarded. Christ, who accomplished the New Covenant by his sacrifice on the cross, is a man. In those actions that "demand the character of ordination and in which Christ himself, the author of the Covenant, the Bridegroom and Head of the Church, is represented, exercising his ministry of salvation . . . his role . . . must be taken by a man." This conclusion follows from an argument from "fittingness": Christ chose men as his apostles because it is fitting for a man to take his part, the part of the Bridegroom, in the celebration of the Eucharist, the New Covenant into which he enters with his Bride, the Church.[22]

---

21. See Hosea 1—3 and Jeremiah 2.

22. See my essay, "The Priest as Sacrament of Christ the Bridegroom," *Worship* 66:6 (November 1992): 498–517.

In the context of this argument, and in the course of responding to an objection sometimes put to it, the declaration comments on the importance of sex in determining one's identity as a person. Sex is significant because it is "directly ordained both for the communion of persons and for the generation of human beings." This is why God created humans "male and female" from the beginning (see Genesis 1:27). The declaration explicitly rejects the view that maleness implies the "superiority" of men over women in the order of values. Instead, it interprets Christ's maleness in terms of "a difference of fact [between the sexes] on the level of functions and services." When the declaration appeals to the "sacramental" signification of sexual difference in its argument that a man is a fitting symbol of Christ, it explains this in terms of the "Bridegroom" motif as it applies to Christ in his covenant with the Church.

THE CONTRIBUTIONS OF POPE JOHN PAUL II

In *Mulieris dignitatem*, Pope John Paul II reasserts the significance of the maleness of Christ in light of the covenant as a "nuptial mystery": a man is the proper symbol of the Bridegroom in relation to the Bride. The Pope's very synthetic meditation on the "great analogy" found in the letter to the Ephesians explores these themes and relates them to the Eucharist. In *Pastores dabo vobis*, he advances the argument by weaving the symbolism of the Bridegroom into a presentation on the vocation of the priest as one configured to Christ as he "faces" the Church, his Bride. These two documents of the papal magisterium, then, spell out further the "theological arguments" of *Inter insigniores*.

The Covenant, the "Great Analogy," and the Eucharist

In *Mulieris dignitatem*, Pope John Paul II reasserts the centrality of the covenant in biblical revelation.[23] He proposes a "meditation" on this theme within his consideration of the analogy in the letter to the Ephesians (5:21–32) that compares the relationship of Christ and the Church to the sacrament of Marriage, and vice versa. He takes special

---

23. *Mulieris dignitatem*, 3–4 and 11, also recalls that in a patristic reading of Genesis 3:15, God's promise of victory over sin and death involved a "woman," and that the New Covenant of God with humanity began with a woman, the Virgin Mary.

note of the reference in Ephesians 5:23 to the biblical account of Creation and the institution of the sacrament of Marriage (see Genesis 2:24); the "unity of the two" in the sacrament of Marriage has its counterpart in the unity of Christ and the Church.

He recalls that this imagery has a precedent in the prophetic literature of the Old Testament. God's covenant with his Chosen People is portrayed as a "marriage," and God himself as the loving husband, for example, in this passage from the prophet Isaiah (54:4–8, 10):

> Your Maker is your husband, the Lord of hosts is his name. . . . For the Lord has called you like a wife forsaken and grieved in spirit. . . . With everlasting love I will have compassion on you, says the Lord. . . . For the mountains may depart and the hills be removed, but my steadfast love shall not depart from you.[24]

The Pope points out that God, speaking through the prophet, can use human language of himself because man and woman are created in the divine image.[25] Here, divine love "is expressed by the analogy of a man's love for a woman."

The same motif is carried forward in the New Testament, but here it is Jesus who is the "Bridegroom," a title that implies his messianic and divine identity. In the Fourth Gospel, John the Baptist confesses that "he who has the bride [Jesus] is the bridegroom" (John 3:27–29). John is not "the Christ," that is, the Messiah, but only the "friend of the bridegroom." In Mark 2:19–20 (and parallels), Jesus is seen using this title of himself; he explains that his disciples do not fast because "they have the bridegroom with them." Saint Paul adopts the same imagery when he warns the members of the Corinthian Church that he feels a "divine jealousy" regarding them, "for I betrothed you to Christ to present you as a pure bride to her one husband" (2 Corinthians 11:2).

The principal New Testament source for this theme, however, is Ephesians 5. Here, Christ and the Church are explicitly identified as Bridegroom and Bride. There is a "great mystery"[26] in the analogy between a man's love for a woman and Christ's love for the Church.

---

24. To the Old Testament passages cited by *Inter insigniores, Mulieris dignitatem* adds Ezekiel 16:8, Isaiah 50:1, and Isaiah 54:5–8.

25. Ibid. Chapter three examines this theme at length.

26. Ibid. See also *Gaudium et spes*, 48, and CCC, 1611–1612, 1617, 1621.

Christ is both Head and Bridegroom of the Church. He "loved the Church and gave himself up for her that he might sanctify her" (Ephesians 5:25). By his gift of self on the cross, Jesus accomplished the New Covenant. His "headship," then, is demonstrated by laying down his life.[27] The Church loved by Christ is joined to him as a wife to her husband: "the two shall become one flesh" (Genesis 2:24). Redemptive love is thereby revealed as spousal love; it is embodied in the "one flesh" of the covenant.

The analogy between the sacrament of Marriage and the Christ-Church relationship, which entails both a likeness and also a certain "non-likeness," is based on the presence of a masculine and a feminine element. The likeness lies first of all in the "spousal" character of God's redemptive love. The symbol of the Bridegroom is masculine. That the Son of God became incarnate as "true man, a male [*homo verus, mas*]," then, has a symbolic connection with the divine economy that culminates in the covenant: "This masculine symbol represents the human aspect of the divine love which God has for Israel, for the Church, and for all people."[28] The "non-likeness" lies in the fact that the "Bride" (Israel, the Church) is a not an individual person but a collective subject, a community composed of both men and women. The Bride-Church, representing redeemed humanity, is the "feminine" element in the analogy. The "Bride" in this case is a "corporate personality," in keeping with a long tradition of regarding the Church as feminine.[29]

Pope John Paul II, with the intention of confirming the teaching of *Inter insigniores*,[30] spells out how the mystery of our redemption, which is a "nuptial mystery" because it brings about the New Covenant, is related to the Eucharist. He calls the Eucharist "the Sacrament of the Bridegroom and the Bride," for it makes present in a sacramental way the sacrifice of Christ the Bridegroom—his body

---

27. *Mulieris dignitatem*, 24, contrasts this interpretation of "headship" with the idea that a husband is the "lord" over his wife with the right to "dominate" her.

28. Ibid., 25. Corresponding to this, all human beings are called to belong to the Church, symbolized as the Bride.

29. For this, see Henri de Lubac, *The Motherhood of the Church* (San Francisco: Ignatius Press, 1982) and *The Splendor of the Church* (New York: Sheed and Ward, 1956), chapter 9.

30. *Mulieris dignitatem*, 26. Note that the Pope restates the "fundamental reasons." He also confirms this teaching in *Christifideles laici*, 49–51.

is given and his blood is poured out—and calls forth the "Bride's" response of love.

Masculinity and femininity, in this analogy, call to mind the dynamics of interpersonal relationship in the sacrament of Marriage, especially the relationship of love, given and reciprocated. The Word's Incarnation according to the male sex, then, symbolizes God's divine love in a human way, and the biblical depiction of the Church as his Bride symbolizes the human response to that love. According to the Pope, the celebration of the Eucharist can be seen to express "the redemptive act of Christ the Bridegroom toward the Church the Bride." The Pope finds this identified in Ephesians: "Christ loved the Church and gave himself up for her" (5:25). And it is this mystery that is sacramentally represented in the Eucharist by the priest, acting *in persona Christi*. The sign of Christ the Bridegroom is clear and unambiguous, the Pope asserts, when the sacramental ministry is performed by a man.

It is legitimate to conclude, Pope John Paul II writes, that in confiding the ministerial priesthood to men, Christ "wished to express the relationship between man and woman, between what is 'feminine' and what is 'masculine.'"[31] He reasons that the Lord, acting with sovereign freedom, linked the institution of the Eucharist directly to the priestly service of the apostles when he charged them to "Do this in remembrance of me" (Luke 22:19). Thus, the relationship between what is "masculine" and what is "feminine," a relationship "willed by God both in the mystery of creation and in the mystery of Redemption," is also expressed sacramentally in the Eucharist.

In the remainder of *Mulieris dignitatem*, John Paul keeps an eye on the analogy that compares the relationship between husband and wife with that between the priest, who acts *in persona Christi*, and the rest of the baptized. In both cases there is a certain "complementarity," that is, a difference ordered to communion, a "unity of the two." By virtue of the common priesthood of the baptized, the "Bride" "responds with the gift of love to the gift of the Bridegroom."[32]

---

31. *Mulieris dignitatem*, 26.
32. Ibid., 27.

The Priest Is a "Living Image" of Christ the Bridegroom

In *Pastores dabo vobis,* Pope John Paul II sets out the doctrine of the ministerial priesthood. Although he does not formally address the significance of maleness, either for Jesus Christ, or for the priest, he does incorporate the motif of Christ as Bridegroom into his consideration of the priesthood in a way that sheds light on our topic.

Pastores dabo vobis asserts that the primary point of reference for the identity of the priest is Christological. By his ordination, the priest is configured to Christ the Head and Shepherd of the Church. He is taken into a new relationship with Christ, and by reason of sharing in his office as Head and Shepherd the priest also assumes a new relationship with the rest of the baptized, Christ's body and his flock. In other words, he becomes a sacramental sign of Christ vis-à-vis, or in relation to, the Church.

To these familiar pairs—Head and body, Shepherd and flock—the Pope adds "Bridegroom and Bride." "The priest," he writes, "is called to be the living image of Jesus Christ, the spouse of the Church."[33] *Pastores dabo vobis* introduces this motif explicitly into the doctrine of the priesthood in a way that builds on the teaching of the Second Vatican Council. For the Council, the ministerial priest (and preeminently the bishop) is the sacramental representative of Christ the Head vis-à-vis his body and Christ the Shepherd vis-à-vis his flock. These biblical analogies entail a relationship, but it is not an interpersonal relationship. The Head-body comparison suggests the organic unity of a single person, and the Shepherd-flock comparison uses a corporate, but non-personal image to portray the Church.

Pastores dabo vobis augments these biblical analogies, expanding "Head" to include "Servant," and "Shepherd" to include "Bridegroom."[34] Being "Head" implies having authority over others, but Jesus exercised his headship in the manner of the Suffering Servant of God; he came "not to be served, but to serve, and to give his life as a ransom for many" (Mark 10:45). So also, the Good Shepherd lays down his life for his sheep (John 10:11), and the Bridegroom loves and gives up his life for his Bride (Ephesians 5:25). The Church is Christ's "personal" counterpart, his beloved "Bride,"

---

33. *Pastores dabo vobis,* 22.
34. Ibid., 21–23.

whom he cleanses "by the washing of water with the word" (5:26) and whom he "nourishes" and "cherishes" (5:29). These four images— Head, Servant, Shepherd, and Bridegroom—all speak of Christ's total gift of self to the Church. To be configured to Christ precisely in his relationship to the Church, the priest must likewise be animated by "pastoral charity," ready to give his life in sacrificial love for Christ's Bride, the Church.

According to John Paul II, the priest's fundamental relationship is to Jesus Christ, but inscribed within this is a relationship to the Church.[35] This means that the priest not only represents Christ, at the head of the community, "facing" God the Father on its behalf; he also represents Christ "facing" the Church as her Bridegroom.[36] Within the Church, and to promote the full exercise of the priesthood of the baptized, he makes Christ's own presence and ministry visible and effective. The priest is not only *in* the Church; he also stands *in relation to* the Church.[37] This is what ordination adds to Baptism. By reason of his Baptism, a priest is *in* the Church. He shares in the common priesthood. He belongs to the community along with his sisters and brothers. Insofar as only a baptized Christian is eligible for priestly ordination, it can be said that Baptism grounds priestly identity. By reason of his ordination, however, a priest is, in addition, placed *in relation to* the Church. As the sacramental representative of Jesus Christ in his role as Head, Shepherd, and Bridegroom of the Church, he "faces" the rest of the baptized.

The Pope clearly intends this reflection to support and illuminate the tradition of reserving priestly ordination to men. He recalls that the priesthood belongs to the constitution, or apostolic structure, of the Church, and that it can be traced back to the Lord's call of the apostles. The priesthood has its origin, however, not only in the ministry of the apostles, but also in the mission of Jesus himself. The foundation of priestly identity, therefore, is Christological. Those ordained to the apostolic ministry, the priesthood, are to represent him and carry on his ministry in the Church. In the structure of the

---

35. Ibid., 16.

36. Ibid., 22.

37. Ibid., 16. The expression "in the forefront" of the Church fails to capture the idea that in taking Christ's role he is "face to face" with the rest of the baptized. For more on this, see de Lubac, *The Motherhood of the Church*, 353–354.

Church, and preeminently in the celebration of the Eucharist, the priest "appears as a sign of the absolute priority and gratuitousness of the grace given to the Church by the risen Christ."[38]

In *Mulieris dignitatem,* on the basis of his analysis of Ephesians 5:21–22, the Pope teaches that "Christ confided this ministry to men in order to symbolize his nuptial relationship with the Church." In *Pastores dabo vobis,* he teaches that ordination incorporates the priest into Christ's own relationship to the Church, making him the sacramental sign of his effective presence and ministry as Bridegroom vis-à-vis the Church as Bride.

THE MINISTERIAL PRIESTHOOD AND NUPTIAL SYMBOLISM

The "theological argument" advanced by the magisterium takes its force from the conviction that the priest is an image of Christ face to face with the Church, and this, preeminently in the celebration of the Eucharist, the sacrifice of the New Covenant. The nuptial imagery in both Testaments relies on the notion that the covenant of God with his people and Christ with the Church is a "unity of the two" brought about by the divine Bridegroom's free initiative and the Bride's free response. The covenant is the "pact" or marriage bond effected by the mutual self-gift. Because the scriptures depict God and Christ in the role of the Bridegroom, a role exclusive to men, it is fitting for a man to be the sacramental sign of Christ, who was and remains a man, in this relationship. The priest acts in the person of the Bridegroom with respect to the Bride-Church in the celebration of the sacrifice of the New Covenant.

This argument from analogy has many facets. Starting from the conviction that priestly ordination is reserved to males on the basis of Christ's will, known by way of his choice of 12 men who stand at the origin of the ordained ministry, it proposes that the meaning of his choice can be grasped in terms of the New Covenant. What is only an analogy in the Old Testament (God's love is compared to that of a Bridegroom) is given concrete historical expression in the Incarnation,

---

38. *Pastores dabo vobis,* 17.

for the Lord Jesus takes on flesh as a man, not a woman. The "Bride-Church," of course, is a corporate personality, not an individual, but this does not empty the nuptial symbolism of meaning nor challenge the reasonableness of requiring that only men represent the Bridegroom in the covenant relationship.

This step in the argument presupposes that the ministerial priesthood is different in kind and not only in degree from the common priesthood. Only if this is true does the ordained priest take the part of the Bridegroom vis-à-vis the Bride, and the other baptized, exercising their common priesthood, take that of the Bride vis-à-vis the Bridegroom. There is, in fact, a certain correlation between the two ways of sharing in Christ's priesthood, the ministerial and the common priesthood,[39] and the two ways in which a man and a woman participate in the marital covenant.[40] This correlation points up how sexual complementarity and its sacramental symbolism shed light on the matter. The New Covenant is a mystery of divine and human freedom, and the covenant itself as a marriage bond, a bond of love. It is a "unity of the two," that is, two distinct partners become "one flesh" as a result of their mutual self-donation. The symbol draws on the dynamics of marital love: the husband's initiative and the wife's response are taken as a paradigm of the initiative of divine grace and the human response.

The magisterium is aware, of course, that some "theological arguments" put forward to explain the reservation of priestly ordination to men have relied on the conviction that as compared to a woman, a man has superior mental and physical strength, and that male headship signifies a man's social preeminence, and his role as "patriarch" of the family. Character traits appropriate to public leadership roles have been assigned exclusively to men and denied to women, and some have proposed that women are not suited to the priestly office on these grounds. But the magisterium has abandoned arguments like these as incompatible with the equality and dignity of women with men. The Christological argument it supplies to illustrate the fittingness of

---

39. Saint Augustine's saying ("For you I am a bishop, with you I am a Christian") is often cited. See *Pastores dabo vobis*, 20.

40. See John McDade, "Gender Matters: Women and Priesthood," *The Month* 255 (July 1994): 254–259.

reserving priestly ordination to men is constructed instead on a biblical analogy. It is interpreted by means of a doctrine of Christian anthropology that takes women's dignity with utmost seriousness and maintains, at the same time, that the complementarity of the sexes is sacramentally significant. This Christological argument employs the symbolism of sexual difference, drawn from the non-interchangeable roles of husband and wife, to illustrate the mystery of the New Covenant and the priest's sacramental representation of the Bridegroom, Head, and Author of the covenant in the celebration of the Eucharist.

Chapter 6

More Objections to the Church's Teaching

We have now set out in some detail both the fundamental reasons and the theological arguments proposed by the contemporary magisterium. The former constitute the basis for its determination that the Church does not have the authority to confer priestly ordination on women. They are set forth as decisive. The latter arguments are offered to illustrate the "fittingness" or meaningfulness of the Lord's dispensation—to elucidate the tradition, not to demonstrate it.

We have already replied to three objections,[1] but now we are in a position to consider several others. We will take up objections to the fundamental reasons first, and then look at selected objections to the theological arguments.

OBJECTIONS TO THE FUNDAMENTAL REASONS

Some critics reject the magisterium's reasoning because they find no New Testament support for the belief that in choosing the Twelve the Lord intended to establish a ministerial priesthood distinct from the priesthood of the baptized. Others claim that women were initially active in the apostolic ministry, according to Jesus' plan for a "discipleship of equals," but that the early Church abandoned this plan. In both cases, the critics privilege the findings of historical scholarship over the witness of the tradition, and their conclusions deviate from the "settled doctrine" of the Catholic Church.

---

1. See chapter three.

Objection 4: Jesus' Choice of Twelve Men Is Irrelevant

Some contemporary exegetes deny that Jesus' choice of men to belong to "the Twelve" has any bearing on the admission of women to priestly ordination. In the first place, they maintain that the Twelve had no successors. Jesus appointed the Twelve to symbolize the "ingathering" of the people of Israel; if he chose only men, it was because they represented the 12 patriarchs, who were male. After the Resurrection, Judas had to be replaced in order that the Twelve would be intact as a group to bear witness to him after the outpouring of the Holy Spirit, but beyond that, members of the group were not replaced. In their eschatological role as judges of the 12 tribes (see Matthew 19:28), the Twelve can have no successors.[2] On these and similar grounds, they hold that there is no ongoing representation of the Twelve in the Church; they are involved in its foundation and at the eschaton, but that is all.

Those who pose this objection actually introduce a still more serious problem, because they deny that the Lord's choice of the Twelve (quite apart from the fact that they were males) reveals his will for the ordained ministry. Anglican New Testament scholar Reginald H. Fuller expresses this widespread consensus when he writes the following:

> When the early church came to work out its arrangements for the ministry it did so *without reference to what Jesus had done in his earthly life.* They proceeded under the guidance of the Spirit. That Jesus appointed only males among the Twelve says nothing about the ministry of the church in the period immediately after Easter.[3]

Fuller also expresses a widely held consensus when he indicates that "it is impossible to draw a direct line of continuity between the Twelve and the second century presbyterate and episcopate."[4] The critics

---

2. See Elisabeth Schüssler Fiorenza, *Discipleship of Equals: A Critical Feminist Ekklesia-logy of Liberation* (New York: Crossroad, 1993), 104–116.

3. "Pro and Con: The Ordination of Women in the New Testament," in *Toward a New Theology of Ordination,* ed. Marianne H. Micks and Charles P. Price (Cambridge, Massachusetts: Greeno and Hadden, 1976): 1–11, at 2.

4. *Pro and Con the Ordination of Women* (New York: Seabury Professional Services, 1976), 61. By citing Fuller's statements from 1976, we mean to recall how these convictions functioned in the debate. The larger critical question has to do with the dominical institution of the apostolic ministry and the foundation of the Church. This objection continues to be posed by Roman Catholic theologians like Peter Hünermann. See "A theologian's dilemma on women priests,"

who hold these views may accept the emergence of "bishops" (*episkopoi*, literally, "overseers") and "presbyters" (*presbyteroi*, literally, "elders") in the subapostolic period as the work of the Holy Spirit, and even as a development necessary for the pastoral care and good order of the Church of God. They do not, however, think of these offices as linked to the ministry initially entrusted by the Lord to the Twelve, or as an "apostolic charge" transmitted by a laying on of hands in a tradition of "apostolic succession."

Reply. The magisterium claims that the Twelve were also called to represent Jesus, and sent out to act in his name and continue his ministry among the messianic people.[5] *Inter insigniores* concedes that the evidence from the Gospel tradition does not make it "immediately obvious" that the Lord intended to entrust the "apostolic charge" only to men; still, it finds that "a number of convergent indications" support this conclusion.[6] In any event, "a purely historical exegesis of the texts cannot suffice" to establish Christ's will on this matter.[7] The Church must consult the tradition, and the tradition sees in his example with respect to the Twelve an expression of his will for the ordained ministry. According to the *Commentary*, "keeping to the sacred text alone and to the points of the history of Christian origins that can be obtained by analyzing that text by itself would be to go back four centuries and find oneself once more amid the controversies of the Reformation."[8]

The Tablet 248 (3 September 1994): 1114–1115, by Peter Hebblethwaite. For a critical assessment of Hünermann's criteriology, see Gerhard Ludwig Müller, *Priesthood and Diaconate* (San Francisco: Ignatius Press, 2002), 38.

5. *Commentary,* 63. The International Theological Commission responded to these challenges in "The Priestly Ministry" (1970) and "Catholic Teaching on Apostolic Succession" (1973). See *Texts and Documents 1969–1985,* ed. Michael Sharkey (San Francisco: Ignatius Press, 1989), 3–87 and 93–104.

6. For more on these connections, see Mansini "On Affirming a Dominical Intention of a Male Priesthood."

7. *Inter insigniores,* 2.

8. Page 62. According to *Dei verbum,* 9, "the church does not draw its certainty about all revealed truths from the holy scriptures alone." According to Sullivan (pp. 1–16), different evaluations of apostolic succession continue to be "church-dividing." He points out (p. 7) that according to Edward Yarnold the Anglican Communion has shifted toward a Protestant view of Holy Orders.

Objection 5: Women Were "Apostles" in the Early Church

Some critics also charge that the magisterium's uncritical identification of "the Twelve" with "the Apostles" obscures important evidence related to the ministry of women. Scholars agree that "Apostles" is a post-Resurrection designation, and that Luke-Acts is responsible for identifying the "Apostles" with the Twelve. Paul, however, claims to be an "Apostle" because he received his missionary mandate from God the Father and from the risen Lord (Galatians 1:1). In the Pauline letters, other believers—Barnabas and James the "brother of the Lord," for example—were also known by this title, but they were not members of "the Twelve."[9]

This distinction is taken to be pertinent to the question of women's access to priestly ordination by exegetes who believe that a certain "Junia," whom Paul refers to as "outstanding among the Apostles" (Romans 16:7), was a woman. If "Junia" is a woman's name, they contend, it is necessary to revise the traditional assumption that only men were "Apostles." On these grounds, too, they maintain, the choice of men for "the Twelve" does not establish a precedent for the exclusion of women from the apostolic ministry. According to the scholarly reconstruction of Elisabeth Schüssler Fiorenza, prohibitions on women's ministry found in the later books of the New Testament represent a deviation from Jesus' original intention for a "discipleship of equals."[10]

Reply. The magisterium does not dispute the distinction between "the Twelve" and the "Apostles," nor does it insist that the New Testament evidence, on its own, is sufficient to determine whether women might be admitted to priestly ordination. Nevertheless, it maintains that even though women were actively involved in many dimensions of the Church's ministry in the New Testament era, only men received the apostolic charge by a laying on of hands in the apostolic Church.[11]

---

9. See Raymond E. Brown, "The Twelve and the Apostolate," *The New Jerome Biblical Commentary* (Englewood Cliffs, New Jersey: Prentice-Hall, 1989), 1377–1381.

10. For a recent account of the exegetical question, see John P. Meier, *A Marginal Jew: Rethinking the Historical Jesus*, vol. 3 (New York: Doubleday, 2001), 125–197.

11. See Vanhoye, 151–57, at 154. This was also the conclusion reached by the Pontifical Biblical Commission in the 1970s.

Scholars find the feminist reconstruction of Christian origins that relies on the reference to "Junia" vulnerable on several counts:[12] Is it certain that this is a woman's name? Does Paul simply mean that Andronicus and Junia were held in high esteem among those who were apostles? Can one so easily dismiss the witness of the pastoral letters, which have as a dominant theme the call to guard the truth that has been handed on from innovations advanced by false teachers (see 2 Timothy 1:14)? Is it likely that the Church departed so soon from a norm established by Jesus? The theory is both improbable and radical: the idea that the Deutero-Pauline pastoral letters represent an early "falling away" from Jesus' original egalitarian pattern suggests that they are not equally authoritative with the rest of the New Testament, and undermines the claim that the Church existing in history is, in the power of the Holy Spirit, the privileged bearer of God's revelation.

OBJECTIONS TO THE THEOLOGICAL ARGUMENTS

Many theologians, and not just those who have rejected the "fundamental reasons" on other grounds, take issue with the "theological arguments." Setting aside the claim that the tradition has another foundation, they raise questions about the validity of the magisterium's reasoning. Some objections concern questions of ecclesiology and sacramental theology; others have to do with the meaning and theological value of sexual or nuptial symbolism in Christian revelation.

Objection 6: All the Baptized Act *in Persona Christi*

Catholic feminist theologians object that priests are not the only ones called to act *in persona Christi*. They protest that all Christians can "image: Christ, because all "put on" Christ at Baptism (Galatians 3:27) and are called to be conformed to him by lives of personal holiness.[13] They think the declaration's assertion that apart from gender correspondence "it would be more difficult to see in the minister the image of Christ" is insulting to women because they insist that women

---

12. See Joseph A. Fitzmyer, "Fidelity to Jesus and the Ordination of Women," *America* 175:20 (December 28, 1996): 9–12, and Ratzinger, "Introduction," 11–13.

13. See Romans 8:29; 2 Corinthians 3:18; 1 John 3:2.

as well as men can be "Christ-like."[14] Borrowing the technical expression *in persona Christi* from the sacramental theology, the critics change its meaning and equate acting in the person of Christ with acting virtuously, in imitation of Christ.

 Reply. For the Church, *in persona Christi* has to do with the new sacramental configuration to Christ as Head of the Church by which the priest is equipped to act as his minister (and not simply on the basis of his own resources) with respect to the rest of the baptized. He acts not in his own "person," but "in the person of Christ the Head of the Church." While the sacerdotal character imposed by Holy Orders is an invisible, spiritual sign *(res et sacramentum)* that enables him so to act, the meaning becomes perceptible only on the level of the visible sign *(sacramentum tantum)*, which in this case is the male priest as the sacramental sign of Christ.[15] This objection rests on a mistake and ignores the difference in kind between the two ways of sharing in Christ's priesthood.

Objection 7: The Priest Acts *in Persona Ecclesiae*

Another objection proposes that the priest acts *in persona Christi* only because he first acts *in persona Ecclesiae* (in the person of the Church). This argument arises from the study of the liturgical texts and from an interest in reasserting the ecclesial dimension of the ministerial priesthood, that is, in affirming that the one who presides at Eucharist does so because he presides over the Church. The priest is said to represent Christ the Head only insofar as he acts *in persona Ecclesiae,* that is, as the head or president of the liturgical assembly as it faces God the Father. Proponents of this theory see the priest as the "sacrament" of the Church, or of the Church's faith. If the priest is first of all a sacramental sign of the Church, which includes both men and women, they reason, either a man or a woman can fulfill this role.

 Reply. The declaration vigorously opposes this reasoning, insisting that the priest acts first *in persona Christi Capitis Ecclesiae,* and

---

 14. According to Elizabeth A. Johnson (*She Who Is: The Mystery of God in Feminist Theological Discourse* [New York: Crossroad, 1992], 73), "the image of Christ does not lie in sexual similarity to the human man Jesus, but in coherence with the narrative shape of his compassionate, liberating life in the world, through the power of the Spirit."

 15. *Commentary,* 70–72.

only then *in persona Ecclesiae.*[16] The *Commentary* reiterates this, observing that it is one of the crucial points for ecclesiology today. *Pastores dabo vobis* carefully delineates the various relationships the priest has: his fundamental relationship with Christ, as his sacramental representation, and then, intimately linked with this, his relationship with the Church.[17]

The magisterium consistently underlines the priority of the priest's sacramental relationship with Christ, and theologians attempt to account for this.[18] The male priest gives visibility to the presence of Christ "facing" the Church as he renews sacramentally the once-for-all sacrifice of the cross in the midst of an organically structured, internally differentiated priestly community.[19] Only then and on this account does the priest act *in persona Ecclesiae,* facing the Father.[20] "Headship" in Catholic ecclesiology is not the same as "leadership" or "presidency"; it is a theological, not a "parliamentary" concept. If the priest acts first *in persona Ecclesiae,* and on this account on behalf of Christ the Head, the Church's role is not differentiated from Christ's; the one is collapsed into the other.[21] There is no symbolic differentiation, no sacramental symbolization of the "two in one flesh" of the New Covenant. Christ is no longer "face to face" with the Church, and the Church is not visibly dependent on Christ.

Objection 8: Jesus' Sex Has No Theological Significance

According to some feminist theologians, the tradition of reserving priestly ordination to men, by improperly attaching theological significance to Jesus' maleness, distorts the meaning of the Incarnation and reveals a preoccupation with sexual difference supportive of male privilege and oppressive to women. These critics point out correctly that the Incarnation is the mystery of God's assuming our *humanity,* and that while the Christological Councils insisted on the completeness

---

16. *Inter insigniores,* 5, takes note of this theory and rejects it. See the *Commentary,* 72–73. For more, see Donald J. Keefe, "Sacramental Sexuality and the Ordination of Women," *Communio* 5:3 (1978): 228–251.

17. *Pastores dabo vobis,* 15–16.

18. For a careful account of the current debate, see Lawrence J. Welch, "For the Church and within the Church: Priestly Representation," *The Thomist* 65:4 (October 2001): 613–637.

19. See *The Motherhood of the Church,* 353–354.

20. See the *Commentary,* 73.

21. See Keefe, 238–240.

of Christ's humanity, they did not comment on his maleness.[22] Some employ the patristic axiom of "What was not assumed was not redeemed," which originally served to counter the Apollinarian error that his human nature lacked a rational soul, to argue that unless Christ's humanity is somehow "inclusive" of both male and female, women are excluded from redemption.[23] Their point is that women as well as men can "image" Christ as priests, because his male sex is not theologically significant.

Reply. A full response to this challenge is beyond the scope of this book,[24] but the logic of it would be as follows. The Word could not assume a genuine human nature without being either a male or a female. Humanity comes in a "double issue." Although man and woman are equal as persons, they are not identical; according to God's plan, there are two different bodily ways of being human. Considered in their sexual difference, man and woman are ordered to one another. Human sexuality is "directly ordained both for the communion of persons and for the generation of human beings."[25]

The meaning of sexual difference cannot be reduced to a function or to a matter of "reproductive role specialization."[26] It includes that, of course, but the fundamental capacity to generate new life also shapes the way a person is inserted into the world and related to others. Only a man can be a husband and a father; only a woman can be a wife and a mother.[27] These non-interchangeable components of sexual complementarity mark our humanity deeply; they refer to

---

22. According to Sandra M. Schneiders, *(Women and the Word* [New York: Paulist Press, 1986], 56), "the maleness of Jesus is theologically, christologically, and sacramentally irrelevant."

23. The logic is that if women cannot represent Christ in the ministerial priesthood, then Christ, being male, cannot "represent" women in such a way as to be their Savior.

24. For an introduction to the challenge it poses, see Anne E. Carr, "Feminist Views of Christology," *Chicago Studies* 35:2 (August 1996): 128–140. For a response, see Nonna Verna Harrison, "The Maleness of Christ," *St. Vladimir's Theological Quarterly* 42:2 (1998): 111–151.

25. *Inter insigniores*, 5. "In biblical revelation this difference is the effect of God's will from the beginning." God created humans "male and female" (Genesis 1:27).

26. According to Rosemary Radford Ruether, *Sexism and God-Talk* (Boston: Beacon, 1983), 111, "maleness and femaleness exist as reproductive role specialization. There is no necessary (biological) connection between reproductive complementarity and either psychological or social role differentiation."

27. Some "social roles" belong exclusively to women or men. Discrimination on the basis of sex, then, is not always based on stereotypes. Because only women bear children, for example, "motherhood" is not a stereotype.

the fundamental vocation of a man or a woman, as a person, to make the gift of self to God and to others.[28] This truth is captured in the traditional belief that persons consecrated to celibacy exercise a certain "spiritual" fatherhood or motherhood.[29]

One cannot deny that being a male rather than a female was as significant for Jesus as it would be for any of us without calling into question his true humanity. As *Inter insigniores* points out, "in human beings the difference of sex exercises an important influence, much deeper than, for example, ethnic differences."[30] Being a man or a woman has biological, but also psychological and spiritual implications. Considered in their mutual and reciprocal relationship, the sexes are not interchangeable, but constitute two different modes of "being a body"; in the nuptial relationship they bear different functions.

The theological significance of Jesus' maleness can be understood in relation to the nuptial symbolism of the covenant, woven throughout the biblical revelation, which expresses the mystery of divine love. In assessing the significance of Jesus' maleness, feminist theology to date appears to disregard the positive value of sexual symbolism and its potential for disclosing love. Sexual difference, in the divine plan, is ordered not to domination, but to intimacy and fruitfulness.[31]

Objection 9: The Risen Christ Transcends Maleness

Another objection to the magisterium's reasoning claims that "the reality of the Risen Christ" transcends sexuality because all of the baptized, both male and female, are members of his body. Most Catholic feminist theologians do not suggest that all sexuality is suppressed in the eschaton, but some do claim that the risen Christ transcends the

---

28. See my essay, "Embodiment: Women and Men, Equal and Complementary," 33–44.

29. *Mulieris dignitatem*, 20–21.

30. *Inter insigniores*, 5. See *Persona humana (Declaration on Certain Questions on Sexual Ethics)*, 1. According to the *Letter on the Collaboration*, 8, "their equal dignity as persons is realized as physical, psychological and ontological complementarity, giving rise to a harmonious relationship of 'uni-duality,' which only sin and 'the structures of sin' inscribed in culture render potentially conflictual."

31. John McDade, "The Maleness of Jesus" (*The Tablet* 243:7754 [February 25, 1989], 221), writes: "We can ill afford to lose images which afford such a passionate interplay between redemption and human sexual experience."

maleness that characterized him during his earthly sojourn.[32] Sandra
Schneiders writes: "The Christ is not simply the glorified Jesus
animating his body which is the Church. . . . This means that Christ,
in contrast to Jesus, is not male, or more exactly is not exclusively
male."[33] Elizabeth Johnson warns believers against falling victim to
a "naive physicalism that would collapse the totality of the Christ into
the human man Jesus."[34] The limitations that attended Jesus in his
human history are transcended, Schneiders and Johnson claim, in his
eschatological state. As a spiritual or "pneumatological" reality, "the
Christ" includes all who are his own; the whole community of the
baptized is said to share in his "Christhood." As a consequence, the
priest who represents Christ need not be a male.

Reply. This objection appeals to a valuable tradition, rooted in
the New Testament (Acts 9:4), regarding the identification of Christ
and his members, who together make up the *totus Christus,* or "whole
Christ," but the objectors' use of the idea results in driving a wedge
between the historical Jesus and the risen Christ, as if Jesus, having
died, is gone from history, while what remains is "the Christ," an
impersonal (or multi-personal) pneumatological reality. The doctrine
of the Lord's bodily Resurrection and the value of his humanity are
thus called into question.

The objection fails to note that the "whole Christ" is a way of
speaking about the intimate communion between Christ and the
Church that is achieved through love. This communion of Head and
members may, indeed, be represented as resulting in one *mystical person*
(the organic union of Head and body), but that does not imply that
the risen Christ is simply identical with the Church, or vice versa. Why
not? Because the unity is understood in terms of a nuptial symbolism
as the "unity of the two," the "one flesh" *(una caro)* of the sacrament
of Marriage. The analogy of marital communion protects the distinction
between Christ and the Church even while it highlights their unity.[35]
This understanding, instead of making sexual symbolism superfluous,
reveals its meaningfulness.

---

32. This claim is often related to belief in the "whole Christ," the union of Head and
members. See CCC § 795.

33. *Women and the Word,* 54.

34. *She Who Is,* 161.

35. See Pope John Paul II, *Theology of the Body,* 314–318.

Objection 10: Why Not Ordain Only Jewish Males?

There is one more objection to consider. If the reason why priestly ordination is reserved to men is that Jesus chose only *men* as members of the Twelve, why is it not also reserved to *Jews*, since he chose only Jewish men? According to this objection, Jesus' sex has no theological value; it was only one of several "historical particularities" that characterized him and should not be used to determine admission to ordination.

Reply. This question, which may seem naive or facetious, in fact highlights a key element in the magisterium's position, namely, that the Church came to discover the importance of Jesus' way of acting only in the course of responding to innovations in practice that deviated from his example. Theologians, pastors, and Popes denounced the admission of women to priestly functions and ordination whenever this occurred. There is no record of any similar controversy over the admission of non-Jews to the apostolic ministry. Once the conditions had been determined for admitting Gentiles to Baptism and participation in the community (see Acts 15:19–20), any such possible controversy had been precluded. Jewish men, fittingly, had been called to represent the 12 patriarchs in the constitution of the New Covenant,[36] but the Fathers of the Church never thought it necessary to subject the Jewish identity of the Twelve to theological reflection in connection with the Christian priesthood. They did, however, reflect on the theological implications of the call of the Twelve to represent Christ, and on the vocation of their successors, the bishops, to represent both Christ and the Twelve in the midst of the Church.[37] In short, while there is no theological or canonical tradition concerning the admission or exclusion of Gentile converts from priestly functions, there is a tradition concerning the exclusion of women from priestly ordination.

This objection, then, confronts us once more with the role of the tradition. If Christ's choice in this matter is considered normative,

---

36. Some argue that this supports rather than puts into question the conclusion that the Lord's choice of men was deliberate.

37. See Othmar Perler, "L'Évêque, représentant du Christ selon les documents des premiers siècles," *L'Épiscopat et l'Église universelle,* "Unam Sanctam," 39 (Paris: Les Éditions du Cerf, 1962), 166, and Robert Murray, *Symbols of Church and Kingdom: A Study in Early Syriac Tradition* (London: Cambridge University Press, 1975), Chapter V: "Titles Shared by Christ and the Apostles or Bishops," 159–204.

and not simply a historically conditioned element of his human history, it is because there is an ecclesial tradition of practice, and a tradition of appealing to his choice of men, and not women, to belong to the Twelve that developed in response to innovations.[38] The magisterium relies on the tradition in interpreting the witness of the scriptures.

Overall Assessment

Some object to the "fundamental reasons" (objections 3, 4, and 5). They are not convinced that Jesus' choice of men as his apostles was meant to be normative for the ordained ministry, or they dispute the claim that apostolic practice represents fidelity to his will for the Church. In their search for scriptural evidence they rely on critical historical scholarship; when it does not yield certain proof of the Lord's intention, they conclude that the Church has no way of knowing what that intention was. They either give scant attention to the witness of an unbroken tradition, unanimous in the Churches of East and West, or they dismiss it as no more than a human tradition determined by sociocultural considerations related to the status of women. In fact, they do not find in the New Testament evidence that links Christ's choice of 12 men during his earthly ministry in any necessary way to the ministerial priesthood that emerged in later generations. It is evident that these conclusions are incompatible with the Church's settled doctrine.

The magisterium insists that the resources of historical scholarship are not sufficient to resolve these questions. It regards the witness of the tradition as the authentic interpreter of the New Testament evidence.[39] From the beginning, the community of disciples included the Twelve. Jesus called them to share in his ministry and sent them forth to represent him and continue his mission. In various ways, they called other men as bishops, priests and deacons and

---

38. How the ministerial priesthood is connected to the Twelve, and why the Lord's choice is meaningful are questions that enter into consideration only after the fact is established.

39. In "Baptism, Eucharist and Ministry: An Appraisal," *Origins* 17:23 (November 19, 1987): 401.402–416, the Holy See says that the question of God's will for the order of the Church "cannot be answered conclusively as long as questions of who will decide, who will discern God's will in various developments and with what authority are left open" (p. 412).

transmitted the gift of the Holy Spirit to them for the same mission by the laying on of hands.[40] According to the tradition, Jesus' selection of the Twelve functions as the primary norm and point of reference for questions of Church order; their apostolic office is held to be the origin of the hierarchical ministry. As the Church came to understand and classify Holy Orders as a sacrament, the Lord's "institution" of the sacrament was identified with the call and mission of the Twelve, and in particular with the commission given them at the Last Supper. Christ's will for the hierarchical constitution of the Church, in fact, was seen to be expressed in his institution of Holy Orders, the sacrament of apostolic ministry.[41]

Others object to the "theological arguments" (objections 1, 2, and 6–10). In their view, the arguments from analogy are inadequate. "Things could just as well have been arranged differently." "Women are capable of carrying out these functions." "The 'nuptial' symbolism of the covenant is just a metaphor, and only one metaphor among many." "This reasoning places unwarranted emphasis on the maleness of Jesus." These critics generally place the whole burden of proof for the Church's teaching on the arguments from fittingness, but this is a burden they were not meant to carry. The critics reverse the logic of the magisterium's case, which first presents the evidence from scripture and tradition that the Lord chose only men as his apostles, and only subsequently seeks to discover its meaning. Regrettably, this mistake supports the notion that the Church's pastors, motivated by a determination to keep women in subordinate positions, have simply replaced one faulty argument with another.[42]

By calling attention to the place of the ministerial priesthood in the sacramental structure of the Church, these critics have provoked a deep examination of interrelated liturgical, sacramental, and ecclesiological questions. They point up the need to come to grips with the question of "sacramentality" and to deepen the dialogue on the

---

40. See Joseph Ratzinger, "Biblical Foundations of Priesthood," *Origins* 20:19 (October 18, 1990): 310–314.

41. This is the clear teaching of *Lumen gentium*, 18–28.

42. In many respects, feminist theology is built on this mistake. It presumes that the magisterium unjustly excludes women from "leadership positions" on the basis of a faulty view of the complementarity of the sexes. It then traces this exclusion to a hitherto unrecognized, but massive, "patriarchal" distortion of biblical revelation.

place of the priesthood in an ecclesiology of communion. In addition, by calling attention to the question of theological anthropology, feminist critics have prompted a very important theological investigation into the meaning and value of human sexuality. However, what some of them regard as a "theory" of sexual complementarity—and a "faulty" one at that—the magisterium now presents more and more explicitly as a *doctrine:* God created humanity in the divine image: "male and female he created them" (Genesis 1:27). The roots of the sacrament of Marriage are disclosed in the controversy over the theological value to be assigned to Christ's maleness and the place of nuptial symbolism in the economy of salvation. "Man and woman have been *created,* which is to say *willed* by God."[43] Perfect equality as human persons does not cancel out the difference, ordered to communion, and the respective value or "genius" of man and woman.

---

43. CCC § 369.

Chapter 7

Ordinatio Sacerdotalis and the Development of Doctrine

Many Christians believe that the development of doctrine that has taken place with respect to the equal rights and dignity of women with men in the social order and in the Church requires a corresponding development leading to the ordination of women. This was, in effect, the logic that governed the admission of women to the ordained ministry in many Protestant Churches and in the Anglican Communion. This reasoning appeared plausible to Catholic theologians who speculated that the Church's practice might not be a genuine theological tradition, but only an unexamined way of doing things based on an outdated, hierarchical theory of the complementarity of the sexes. Early in the Catholic discussion of the ordination of women, several leading theologians announced that there were no "theological objections" to such a development.[1]

THIS TRADITION IS NOT OPEN TO DEVELOPMENT

Today, many continue to frame the question in the following terms: Is the reservation of priestly ordination to men only a human tradition, open to development under the impulse of the Holy Spirit, or does it belong to the tradition grounded in the will of Christ that remains normative for the life of the Church? And how does the Church determine this?

The reasons for the judgment that the Church has no authority to confer priestly ordination on women have been set forth

---

1. Simon Gaine provides an excellent analysis of the way the various theological arguments have functioned in the history of this question in "Ordination to the Priesthood."

at length, and they demonstrate how the magisterium has, in the concrete, determined the status of this tradition. We might also gain insight, however, by considering this question briefly from the perspective of the development of doctrine, using criteria set out by the Council of Trent and by Cardinal John Henry Newman (1801–1890).

This Tradition Meets the Tridentine Criteria

According to the Council of Trent, responding to the *sola scriptura* principle of the Reformers, traditions may be shown to belong to the *Verbum Dei traditum* ("the word of God handed on as tradition")[2] if they fulfill three criteria. They must "have the Gospel as their source," "have been received by the Apostles from the very mouth of Christ, or have been revealed to them by the Holy Spirit," and "have been preserved without interruption in the Catholic Church."[3] If the practice of reserving priestly ordination to men does not meet this standard it is simply a human tradition, open to further "development," but if it does, it belongs to the tradition, to the deposit of faith.

The magisterium traces the Church's practice of reserving priestly ordination to men to the witness of the Gospels, that is, to the will of Christ made known by his example in choosing only men to belong to the Twelve. It then consults the practice of the apostles and finds that they maintained the same pattern. Only men are reported to have been set aside to fill leadership roles in the apostolic Church by a laying on of hands, and the Deutero-Pauline pastoral epistles clearly indicate that men were chosen to direct the first Christian communities.[4] This tradition, then, meets the first two criteria: it is founded in the Gospels and attested by the witness of the apostolic Church.

The third criterion for determining whether a tradition is of divine rather than merely human origin is that it has been preserved without interruption in the Catholic Church. The tradition of reserving priestly ordination to men was so firm over the course of centuries that until recently the magisterium felt no need to intervene "to formulate a principle which was not attacked, or to defend a law which was not

---

2. *Dei verbum*, 10.
3. Council of Trent, Session IV, (DS, 1501; ND, 210).
4. See Vanhoye, 154.

challenged."[5] Whenever innovations appeared, they were "immediately noted and condemned,"[6] and theologians and canonists "have been almost unanimous in considering this exclusion [of women] as absolute and having a divine origin."[7] That this tradition was not considered to be simply a disciplinary matter, or law of the Church, is seen from the fact that generations of theologians evaluated it as "theologically certain," "proximate to faith," and even "doctrine of faith."[8] Theologians have traditionally agreed, moreover, that the attempted ordination of a woman would be invalid. The tradition of practice has remained unbroken in those Christian communions that maintain a sacramental understanding of priesthood and apostolic succession. Because "the church does not draw its certainty about all revealed truths from the holy scriptures alone,"[9] it is possible to be certain that this tradition belongs to the deposit of faith.

Newman's Theory of Development Confirms This Judgment

We can consider this matter from another angle by using Cardinal Newman's classic theory of the development of doctrine to examine the controversy over the priestly ordination of women from the perspective of its results. Newman's theory arises from his belief that the Christian faith is a living "idea." This "idea" cannot be fully communicated in any proposition, and cannot remain static, but is being constantly "turned over" in the minds of believers and understood in new ways. There is an antecedent probability, then, that doctrines of the faith will develop. This takes place when new questions are raised, new ideas entertained, and erroneous theories proposed and corrected. Given this probability, it is necessary to evaluate the thoughts that emerge from this process.

In *An Essay on the Development of Christian Doctrine*, Newman identifies seven "notes"[10] with which to distinguish an authentic

---

5. *Inter Insigniores*, 1.

6. Ibid.

7. *Commentary*, 61.

8. Ibid.

9. *Dei verbum*, 9.

10. See John Henry Cardinal Newman, *An Essay on the Development of Christian Doctrine* (Notre Dame: University of Notre Dame Press, 1989), 171–206. The "notes" are preservation of type, continuity of principles, power of assimilation, logical sequence, anticipation of its future, conservative action on its past, and chronic vigor.

"development" from its opposite, a "corruption." One of his seven "notes," "conservative action on the past," offers particular help for our case. According to Newman's theory, an authentic development leads to a deeper synthesis of truths already held, whereas a "corruption" leads to the disintegration of what had previously been in possession. In his words,

> A true development [is] one which is conservative of the course of antecedent developments[,] being really those antecedents and something besides them: it is an addition which illustrates, not obscures, corroborates, not corrects, the body of thought from which it proceeds; and this is its characteristic as contrasted with a corruption.[11]

If the proposed "development" requires not just the realignment but also the rejection of doctrines previously held, that proposal is revealed to be a "corruption."

For Newman, it is ultimately the magisterium that is able to judge whether a projected change would be a "development" or a "corruption." In fact, Pope John Paul II has done just this in *Ordinatio sacerdotalis.* He confirmed by his papal authority the tradition that has been in possession "from the beginning" and excluded the possibility that the Church could change it. The development many anticipated cannot take place, he asserts; the practice expresses Christ's will and the Church has no authority to alter it.

We have set out evidence that there has been an authentic development of doctrine with respect to the equal rights and dignity of women with men, and that this has been integrated into Catholic teaching and practice, at least in principle. And we have indicated why, according to the judgment of the magisterium, this development does not lead to the admission of women to the priesthood. As the debate itself has demonstrated, this issue—though apparently a matter of discipline—invariably touches on more fundamental questions of doctrine. In *Ordinatio sacerdotalis,* Pope John Paul II asserts as part of his doctrinal conclusion that this tradition pertains to " the Church's divine constitution."[12] Earlier in the letter, however, he also reports the warning of Pope Paul VI that the question of women's ordination

---

11. Newman, 200.
12. Article 4.

touches on the Church's "Christian anthropology" as well.[13] These are the "settled doctrines" that arguments in favor of women's ordination risk distorting or even denying.

Until the prospect of a development was seriously entertained, many doctrinal connections remained hidden, but the controversy has brought them to light. As the ten objections we have studied reveal, the effort to justify women's ordination has led to the adoption of premises that are at odds with these settled Catholic doctrines. By challenging the tradition that saw a permanent norm for the ministerial priesthood in Christ's call of men, but not women, as apostles, the objections end up questioning the Lord's intention with respect to the priesthood, the Church's hierarchical constitution, and even its foundation. By calling into question the sacramental significance of the complementarity of the sexes, the objections undermine not only the distinction between Christ and his Church, which is given sacramental expression by reserving priestly ordination to men, but also the biblical revelation that God created humanity male and female and saw that it was good. The biblical doctrine that the difference between man and woman is willed by God,[14] and with it the doctrine of Marriage as a sacrament, is thereby put in doubt.

According to Newman's criterion, this illustrates that the proposed "development" is in fact a "corruption." It appears to lead to the disintegration and dismantling of the received tradition, not its consolidation and confirmation. Newman states another principle: in the face of a unanimous and unbroken tradition, the burden of proof rests on those who challenge the Church's teaching, not those who uphold it.[15] The challengers in this case have been unable to prove their point.

The magisterium's defense of the tradition, on the other hand, has led to a new synthesis. Its "theological arguments," in particular, draw various themes into a new constellation: the symbolism of the covenant in which God is likened to the Husband of Israel, Christ's self-identification as the Bridegroom, the identification of the Church

---

13. Article 2.

14. *Letter on the Collaboration of Men and Women*, 5–6, and CCC §§ 369–372.

15. Newman, 120.

as his Bride, and the sacrifice of Christ (and its Eucharistic representation) as the sealing of the New Covenant.[16] These reflections
enrich the Church's understanding of the dynamic interrelation of the
common and the ministerial priesthood in an ecclesiology of
communion. They likewise promote a new appreciation of the "nuptial"
meaning of the body and the sacramental value of the complementarity
of the sexes.

CONCLUSION

The promulgation of *Ordinatio sacerdotalis* has created a new situation,
both within the Catholic community and within the larger Christian
community, for it clearly put to rest the expectation that Catholic
practice will change. Opposition to this teaching continues to be
expressed within the Church, but the new "ecclesial reality" established
by its formal expression favors its reception by Catholics.[17] The
discussion has been declared closed. The Pope clearly intended to
prohibit Catholic theologians, pastors, and religious from publicly
espousing positions contrary to this teaching. This does not mean,
however, that the teaching itself does not need to be expounded and
discussed. Because the magisterium requires "the full and unconditional
assent of the faithful"[18] to this teaching, it devolves on Catholic
theologians to explain this as fully and adequately as they can.

According to *Ordinatio sacerdotalis,* the authentic development
in Catholic doctrine with respect to the status of women in society
and in the Church does not require their admission to the ministerial
priesthood. Closing off this possibility has led the Church to search
for new ways to identify the "genius" of woman and a new commitment
to foster the collaboration of men and women in the Church and
in society.

---

16. We have not even mentioned how this can be coordinated with the doctrine that the
Blessed Virgin Mary is the type of the Church and with the tradition of regarding consecrated
virgins as liturgical symbols of the Church as the Bride of Christ.

17. See Matthieu Wagemaker, *Two Trains Running: The Reception of the Understanding of
Authority by ARCIC I Related to the Debates on the Ordination of Women* (Bern: Peter Lang, 1999),
399–400.

18. See the "presentation" of the apostolic letter, *Origins* 24:4 (June 9, 1994), 53; *From "Inter
Insigniores,"* 194.

Bibliography

Ashley, Benedict. *Justice in the Church: Gender and Participation.* Washington, D.C.: The Catholic University of America Press, 1996.

Baptism, Eucharist, and Ministry. Faith and Order Paper No. 111. Geneva: World Council of Churches, 1982.

"Baptism, Eucharist, and Ministry: An Appraisal," *Origins* 17:23 (November 19, 1987): 401.402–416.

Beauchesne, Richard. "Scriptural/Theological Argument against Women's Ordination (Simply Stated) and Responses," *Journal of Ecumenical Studies* 32:1 (Winter 1995): 107–113.

Bliss, Kathleen. *The Service and Status of Women in the Churches.* London: S.C.M. Press, 1952.

Brown, Raymond E. "The Twelve and the Apostolate," in *The New Jerome Biblical Commentary,* Englewood Cliffs, New Jersey: Prentice-Hall, 1989, §81: 135–157.

Butler, Sara. "Second Thoughts on Ordaining Women," *Worship* 63:2 (March 1989): 157–165.

___. "The Priest as Sacrament of Christ the Bridegroom," *Worship* 66:6 (November 1992): 498–517.

___. "Priestly Identity: 'Sacrament' of Christ the Head," *Worship* 70:4 (July 1996): 290–306.

___. "The Ordination of Women: A New Obstacle to the Recognition of Anglican Orders," *Anglican Theological Review* 78:1 (Winter 1996): 96–113.

___. "Women's Ordination and the Development of Doctrine," *The Thomist* 61 (October 1997): 501–524.

___. "Embodiment: Women and Men, Equal and Complementary," in *The Church Women Want,* 35–44.

Carr, Anne E. "Feminist Views of Christology," *Chicago Studies* 35:2 (August 1996): 128–140.

The Church and the International Women's Year 1975. Vatican City: Pontifical Council for the Laity, 1976.

The Church and Women. Edited by Helmut Moll. San Francisco: Ignatius Press, 1988.

The Church Women Want. Edited by Elizabeth A. Johnson. New York: Crossroad, 2002.

Churches Respond to BEM. Edited by Max Thurian. Vols. 1–6. Geneva: World Council of Churches, 1986–1988.

Congar, Yves M. J. "Bulletin de Théologie: Les ministères—Les femmes et les ministères ordonnés," *Revue des sciences philsophiques et théologiques* 58 (October 1974): 638–642.

___. "Simples Réflexions," *Vie Consacrées* 44 (1972): 310–314.

Congregation for the Doctrine of the Faith, *From "Inter Insigniores" to "Ordinatio Sacerdotalis": Documents and Commentaries.* Washington, D.C.: United States Catholic Conference, 1998.

_____. *Mysterium ecclesiae (Declaration in Defense of the Catholic Doctrine on the Church against Certain Errors of the Present Day)*. Washington, D.C.: United States Catholic Conference, 1973.

_____. *Inter insigniores*. "Vatican Declaration: Women in the Ministerial Priesthood," *Origins* 6:33 (February 3, 1977): 517.519–524. "A Commentary on the Declaration," *Origins* 6:33 (February 3, 1977): 524–531.

_____. "The Minister of the Eucharist," *Origins* 13 (September 15, 1983): 229–233.

_____. "Vatican Says Clarifications Strengthen Agreement," *Origins* 24:17 (October 6, 1994): 299–304, at 303.

_____. "Inadmissibility of Women to Ministerial Priesthood," *Origins* 25:24 (November 30, 1995): 401.403–405.

_____. "Letter on the Collaboration of Men and Women," *Origins* 34:11 (August 26, 2004): 169.171–176.

Congregation for the Evangelization of Peoples, "The Role of Women in Evangelization," *Origins* 5:44 (April 22, 1976): 702–707.

Coyle, J. Kevin. "The Fathers on Women and Women's Ordination," *Église et théologie* 9:1 (January 1978), 51–102.

De Lubac, Henri. *The Motherhood of the Church*. Translated by Sergia Englund. San Francisco: Ignatius Press, 1982.

_____. *The Splendor of the Church*. Translated by Michael Mason. New York: Sheed and Ward, 1956.

Donovan, Daniel. *What Are They Saying About the Ministerial Priesthood?* New York: Paulist Press, 1992.

Dulles, Avery. "Ecumenism without Illusions: A Catholic Perspective," *First Things* No. 4 (June/July 1990): 20–25.

_____. *"Humanae Vitae* and *Ordinatio Sacerdotalis:* Problems of Reception," in *Church Authority in American Culture: The Second Cardinal Bernardin Conference*. New York: Crossroad, 1999, 14–28.

Dunn, Patrick J. *A Re-examination of the Roman Catholic Theology of the Presbyterate*. New York: Alba House, 1990.

Faherty, William B. *The Destiny of Modern Woman in the Light of Papal Teaching*. Westminster, Maryland: Newman Press, 1950.

Fitzmyer, Joseph A. "Fidelity to Jesus and the Ordination of Women," *America* 175:20 (December 28, 1996): 9–12.

Fox, Zeni. *New Ecclesial Ministry: Lay Professionals Serving the Church*. Franklin, Wisconsin: Sheed and Ward, 2002.

Fuller, Reginald. "Pro and Con: The Ordination of Women in the New Testament," in *Toward a New Theology of Ordination*. Edited by Marianne H. Micks and Charles P. Price. Cambridge, Massachusetts: Greeno and Hadden, 1976, 1–11.

Gaine, Simon Francis. "Ordination to the Priesthood: 'That the one who acts in the person of Christ the Head must needs be male but need not be a Jew,'" *New Blackfriars* 83:975 (May 2002): 212–231.

Galot, Jean. *Mission et ministère de la femme*. Paris: Lethielleux, 1973.

Grabowski, John S. "Mutual Submission and Trinitarian Self-Giving," *Angelicum* 74:4 (1997): 489–512.

Harahan, Robert. *The Vocation of Women: The Teaching of the Modern Popes from Leo XIII to Paul VI*. Rome: Pontificia Universitas Laterensis, 1983.

Harrison, Nonna Verna. "The Maleness of Christ," *St. Vladimir's Theological Quarterly* 42:2 (1998): 111–151.

Hauke, Manfred. *Women in the Priesthood? A Systematic Analysis in the Light of the Order of Creation and Redemption.* San Francisco: Ignatius Press, 1988.

Hebblethwaite, Peter. "A Theologian's Dilemma on Women Priests," *The Tablet* 248 (3 September 1994): 1114–1115.

International Theological Commission, "Catholic Teaching on Apostolic Succession," in *Texts and Documents 1969–1985.* San Francisco: Ignatius Press, 1989, 93–104.

___. "The Priestly Ministry," in *Texts and Documents 1969–1985*, 3–87.

International Women's Year 1975 Study Kit. Washington, D.C.: United States Catholic Conference, 1975.

John Paul II, Pope. "John Paul II/'Mulieris Dignitatem,' On the Dignity and Vocation of Women," *Origins* 18:17 (October 6, 1988): 261.263–283.

___. Post-Synodal Apostolic Exhortation *Christifideles Laici (On the Vocation and the Mission of the Lay Faithful in the Church and in the World).* Washington, D.C.: USCC, 1988.

___. *Pastores dabo vobis, Origins* 21:45 (April 16, 1992): 717.719–759.

___. *Ordinatio sacerdotalis.* "Apostolic Letter on Ordination and Women," *Origins* 24:4 (June 9, 1994): 49.51–52.

___. "Letter to Women," *Origins* 25:9 (July 27, 1995): 137.139–143.

Johnson, Elizabeth A. "Imaging God, Embodying Christ: Women as a Sign of the Times," in *The Church Women Want*, 45–59.

___. *She Who Is: The Mystery of God in Feminist Theological Discourse.* New York: Crossroad, 1992.

Keefe, Donald J. "Sacramental Sexuality and the Ordination of Women," *Communio* 5:3 (1978): 228–251.

LaCugna, Catherine Mowry. "Catholic Women as Ministers and Theologians," *America* 167:10 (October 10, 1992): 238–248.

Ligier, Louis. "Women and the Ministerial Priesthood," *Origins* 7:14 (April 20, 1978): 694–702.

Lynch, John E. "The Ordination of Women: Protestant Experience in Ecumenical Perspective," *Journal of Ecumenical Studies* 12:2 (Spring 1975): 173–197.

McDade, John. "Gender Matters: Women and Priesthood," *The Month* 255 (July 1994): 254–259.

___. "The Maleness of Jesus," *The Tablet* 243:7754 (February 25, 1989), 220–221.

McDermott, Rose. *The Legal Condition of Women in the Church: Shifting Policies and Norms.* Canon Law Studies, 499. Washington, D.C.: The Catholic University of America, 1979.

___. "Woman, Canon Law on," in The Catholic University of America, *New Catholic Encyclopedia*, second edition. Farmington Hills, Michigan: Thomson Gale, 2002.

___. "Women in the New Code," *The Way Supplement* 50 (Summer 1984): 27–37.

Mansini, Guy. "Episcopal *Munera* and the Character of Episcopal Order," *The Thomist* 66 (2002): 369–394.

___. "On Affirming a Dominical Intention of a Male Priesthood," *The Thomist* 61:2 (April 1997): 301–316.

___. "Sacerdotal Character at the Second Vatican Council," *The Thomist* 67 (2003): 539–577.

Martin, Francis. Feminist Theology: *The Feminist Question: Feminist Theology in the Light of Christian Tradition.* Grand Rapids, Michigan: William B. Eerdmans, 1994.

Martin, John Hilary. "The Injustice of Not Ordaining Women: A Problem for Medieval Theologians," *Theological Studies* 48:2 (June 1987): 303–316.

____. "The Ordination of Women and the Theologians in the Middle Ages," in *A History of Women and Ordination.* Vol. 1: *The Ordination of Women in a Medieval Context.* Edited by Bernard Cooke and Gary Macy. Lanham, Maryland: Scarecrow Press, 2002, 31–175.

Müller, Gerhard Ludwig. *Priesthood and Diaconate: The Recipient of the Sacrament of Holy Orders from the Perspective of Creation Theology and Christology.* Translated by Michael J. Miller. San Francisco: Ignatius Press, 2002.

Murray, Robert. *Symbols of Church and Kingdom: A Study in Early Syriac Tradition.* London: Cambridge University Press, 1975.

The Nature and Purpose of the Church. Faith and Order Paper 181. Geneva: World Council of Churches, 1998.

Newman, John Henry. *An Essay on the Development of Christian Doctrine.* Notre Dame: University of Notre Dame Press, 1989.

The Order of the Priesthood: Nine Commentaries on the Vatican. Huntington, Indiana: Our Sunday Visitor, 1978.

Paul VI, Pope. "Women/Disciples and Co-Workers," *Origins* 4:45 (May 1, 1975): 718–719.

____. "Women/Balancing Rights and Duties," *Origins* 5:35 (February 19, 1976): 449.551–552.

____. "Women in the Plan of God," *The Pope Speaks* 22 (1977): 124–125.

Perler, Othmar. "L'Évêque, représentant du Christ selon les documents des premiers siècles," *L'Épiscopat et l'Église universelle.* "Unam Sanctam" 39. Paris: Les Éditions du Cerf, 1962.

Pontifical Biblical Commission (unauthorized report). "Can Women Be Priests?" *Origins* 6:6 (July 1, 1976): 92–96.

Pope John Paul II on the Genius of Women. Washington, D.C.: United States Catholic Conference, 1997.

Rahner, Karl. "Women and the Priesthood," in *Concern for the Church.* Theological Investigations XX. New York: Crossroad, 1981, 35–47.

Ratzinger, Joseph. "Biblical Foundations of Priesthood," *Origins* 20:19 (October 18, 1990): 310–314.

____. "Introduction," in *From "Inter Insigniores,"* 5–17.

____. "The Male Priesthood: A Violation of Women's Rights?" *From "Inter Insigniores,"* 142–150.

Research Report: Women in Church and Society. Edited by Sara Butler. Bronx, New York: The Catholic Theological Society of America, 1978.

Reynolds, Nancy. *A Comparison of the Specific Juridic Status of Women in the 1917 and 1983 Codes of Canon Law.* Canon Law Studies. Washington, D.C.: The Catholic University of America, 1984.

Rezette, Jean. "La Sacerdoce et la Femme chez Saint Bonaventure," *Antonianum* 51:4 (October-December 1976): 520–527.

Ruether, Rosemary Radford. *Sexism and God-Talk: Toward a Feminist Theology.* Boston: Beacon, 1983.

Schneiders, Sandra M. *Beyond Patching: Faith and Feminism in the Catholic Church.* Revised edition. New York: Paulist Press, 2004.

___. *Women and the Word.* New York: Paulist Press, 1986.

Schüssler Fiorenza, Elisabeth. "Word, Spirit, and Power," in *Women of Spirit.* Edited by Eleanor McLaughlin and Rosemary Ruether. Boston: Beacon Press, 1979, 29–70.

___. *In Memory of Her: A Feminist Theological Reconstruction of Christian Origins.* New York: Crossroad, 1984.

___. *Discipleship of Equals: A Critical Feminist Ekklesia-logy of Liberation.* New York: Crossroad, 1993.

Steinfels, Peter. *A People Adrift: The Crisis of the Roman Catholic Church in America.* New York: Simon and Schuster, 2003.

Stendahl, Krister. *The Bible and the Role of Women.* Philadelphia: Fortress, 1966.

Sullivan, Francis A. *From Apostles to Bishops: The Development of the Episcopacy in the Early Church.* New York: The Newman Press, 2000.

The Theology of the Body according to John Paul II: Human Love in the Divine Plan. With a foreword by John S. Grabowski. Boston: Pauline Books and Media, 1997.

Thomas Aquinas, Saint. *Summa Theologiae Supplement,* question 39.

Van der Meer, Haye. *Women Priests in the Catholic Church?* Translated by Arlene and Leonard Swidler. Temple University Press, 1973 (German original, *Priestertum der Frau?,* 1969).

Vanhoye, Albert. "Church's Practice in Continuity with New Testament Teaching," in *From Inter Insigniores,* 151–157.

Wagemaker, Matthieu. *Two Trains Running: The Reception of the Understanding of Authority by ARCIC I Related to the Debates on the Ordination of Women.* Bern: Peter Lang, 1999.

Welch, Lawrence J. "For the Church and within the Church: Priestly Representation," *The Thomist* 65:4 (October 2001): 613–637.

Women and Jurisdiction: An Unfolding Reality—The LCWR Study of Selected Church Leadership Roles. Edited by Anne Munley et al. Silver Spring, Maryland: Leadership Conference of Women Religious, 2002.

Women in Christ: Toward a New Feminism. Edited by Michele M. Schumacher. Grand Rapids, Michigan: Wm. B. Eerdmans, 2004.

Index

About the Liturgical Institute

The Liturgical Institute, founded in 2000 by His Eminence Francis Cardinal George of Chicago, offers a variety of options for education in Liturgical Studies. A unified, rites-based core curriculum constitutes the foundation of the program, providing integrated and balanced studies toward the advancement of the renewal promoted by the Second Vatican Council. The musical, artistic, and architectural dimensions of worship are given particular emphasis in the curriculum. Institute students are encouraged to participate in its "liturgical heart" of daily Mass and Morning and Evening Prayer. The academic program of the Institute serves a diverse, international student population—laity, religious, and clergy—who are preparing for service in parishes, dioceses, and religious communities. Personalized mentoring is provided in view of each student's ministerial and professional goals. The Institute is housed on the campus of the University of St. Mary of the Lake/Mundelein Seminary, which offers the largest priestly formation program in the United States and is the center of the permanent diaconate and lay ministry training programs of the Archdiocese of Chicago. In addition, the University has the distinction of being the first chartered institution of higher learning in Chicago (1844), and one of only seven pontifical faculties in North America.

For more information about the Liturgical Institute and its programs, contact: usml.edu/liturgicalinstitute. Phone: 847-837-4542. E-mail: litinst@usml.edu.

Msgr. Reynold Hillenbrand
1904-1979

Monsignor Reynold Hillenbrand, ordained a priest by Cardinal George Mundelein in 1929, was Rector of St. Mary of the Lake Seminary from 1936 to 1944.

He was a leading figure in the liturgical and social action movement in the United States during the 1930s and worked to promote active, intelligent, and informed participation in the Church's liturgy.

He believed that a reconstruction of society would occur as a result of the renewal of the Christian spirit, whose source and center is the liturgy.

Hillenbrand taught that, since the ultimate purpose of Catholic action is to Christianize society, the renewal of the liturgy must undoubtedly play the key role in achieving this goal.

Hillenbrand Books strives to reflect the spirit of Monsignor Reynold Hillenbrand's pioneering work by making available innovative and scholarly resources that advance the liturgical and sacramental life of the Church.